# Rethinking Rehabilitation

# Rethinking Rehabilitation
## Why Can't We Reform Our Criminals?

*David Farabee*

The AEI Press

*Publisher for the American Enterprise Institute*

WASHINGTON, D.C.

Distributed to the Trade by National Book Network, 15200 NBN Way, Blue Ridge Summit, PA 17214. To order call toll free 1-800-462-6420 or 1-717-794-3800. For all other inquiries please contact the AEI Press, 1150 Seventeenth Street, NW, Washington, DC 20036 or call 1-800-862-5801.

This publication is a project of the National Research Initiative, a program of the American Enterprise Institute that is designed to support, publish, and disseminate research by university-based scholars and other independent researchers who are engaged in the exploration of important public policy issues.

Library of Congress Cataloging-in-Publication Data

Farabee, David
  Rethinking rehabilitation : why can't we reform our criminals? /
    David Farabee.
    p. cm.
  Includes bibliographical references.
  ISBN 0-8447-7190-2 (pbk. : alk. paper)
1. Criminals—Rehabilitation—United States. 2. Criminal justice, Administration of—United States. 3. Criminal justice, Administration of—United States—Evaluation. 4. Correctional Institutions—United States. 5. Imprisonment—United States. 6. Parole—United States. I. Title.

  HV9304.F37 2005
  364.6'01—dc22

                             2004026949

10  09  08  07  06  05        2  3  4  5  6  7

*Printed in the United States of America*

*In memory of my father, James M. Farabee*

# Contents

# Foreword

*The great tragedy of Science—the slaying of a beautiful hypothesis by an ugly fact.*

—Thomas Henry Huxley, 1870

I wish it were otherwise, but scientific evidence is sorely lacking to support the effectiveness of rehabilitation programs for criminal offenders. It is similarly lacking to support the effectiveness of most programs aimed at treating conditions that exacerbate crime, such as substance abuse and dependence. Although a limited menu of behavioral and pharmacological treatments have shown small to moderate effects among offenders when administered under controlled research conditions, those effects tend to decline rapidly soon after criminal justice supervision is withdrawn. Moreover, these empirically validated interventions are almost entirely unavailable to offenders in day-to-day practice. The vast majority of services for offenders and substance abusers in this country are group-based, peer-administered, and loosely modeled on an amalgam of psycho-educational and twelve-step principles. Typically, the "ingredients" or "mechanisms of action" of these interventions are so vaguely defined as to be essentially unmeasurable, unverifiable, and unfalsifiable. And because the interventions are rarely, if ever, standardized or systematized, they are delivered quite differently across different programs, making it nearly impossible to discern the effects of such an elusive target.

Even if evidence-based treatments were available in practice, there is serious question whether the rehabilitation system could begin to support and diffuse them effectively for offenders. With approximately 40 percent of community-based programs being closed or reorganized nearly every two years, and with approximately 50 percent staff turnover per year among administrators and clinicians, how can the programs maintain the level of skills necessary to deliver comprehensive services to a seriously disadvantaged population? And given that between one-quarter and one-half of the service providers nationally have no more than a two-year college associate's degree, how could they reasonably be expected to master the complicated principles and techniques required to intervene in chronic and intransigent conditions such as crime and addiction?

Finally, were we to upgrade our rehabilitation system in terms of skills and personnel, the question would remain whether the target population is remotely interested in receiving the interventions. Even when the available data are cast in the most favorable light, between 40 and 70 percent of offenders fail to comply *minimally* with treatment conditions imposed on them, and fewer than 10 percent complete a prescribed regimen. Perhaps—just perhaps—they don't all really desire rehabilitation.

There are two paths one can take in response to these discomfiting facts. One path is to marshal evidence—*any* evidence—to support the utility of rehabilitation efforts. One could, for example, report outcomes only for program graduates; that is, identify the most successful cases after the fact, and then act as if those were the only individuals the program was ever truly interested in. Similarly, one could relate tenure in treatment to outcomes, and then erroneously conclude from this biased correlation that treatment "caused" better outcomes. This optimistic path has the decided advantage of raising clients' hopes for success, and encouraging funding agencies and third-party payers to continue subsidizing treatment and research efforts. On the downside, however, it can also thwart progress and stunt creativity. If services are basically fine as they are, then future efforts should simply do more of the same for a longer period of time.

An alternative path is to call attention to the "elephant in the room." This path risks further stigmatization of offenders and pessimism about future endeavors. On the other hand, it can also spur the field to think more realistically and creatively about the difficult tasks at hand. Paradigm shifts are nearly always precipitated by poignantly disappointing evidence. Recently, just such a paradigm shift triggered the promising advent of drug courts, when a group of criminal-court judges became fed up with the unacceptable state of affairs in community probation and drug treatment.

In this volume, David Farabee travels farther down this latter path. He exposes many of the "tricks of the trade" used by evaluators and advocates to "shine" disappointing findings, and raises provocative questions about the basic logic underlying current rehabilitative efforts. In so doing, he risks the same vilification for apostasy that befell the late Robert Martinson, who was scapegoated for heralding the "nothing works" philosophy that ended the last rehabilitation era. This, however, would be an inaccurate portrayal of Dr. Farabee's position. As I read his incisive arguments, Dr. Farabee is not inviting another swing of the pendulum toward one-dimensional, law-and-order tactics. He recognizes that all single-minded strategies, whether they bear a liberal or conservative stamp, have been equally exposed as impotent by an honest appraisal of the research evidence. He challenges us, rather, to think beyond the intellectual confines of "treat them" versus "punish them." He asks us to adopt the scientific method as our guide for determining which practices to keep, which to discard, and which to adapt to new functions.

It behooves the field to heed this advice and to stop defending the unsustainable status quo. The sad truth is that we have not, as yet, identified an effective range of strategies for offenders, and we will never do so if we keep trying to finesse this fact. As treatment providers are wont to say, the first step toward a cure is acknowledging the existence of a problem. This monograph takes that first step.

Douglas B. Marlowe, JD, PhD
Treatment Research Institute
at the University of Pennsylvania

# Acknowledgments

I am indebted to my friends and colleagues Stephen James, Doug Marlowe, Michael Prendergast, and Sally Satel for their comments on drafts of this monograph; thanks also to Montgomery Brown, Samuel Thernstrom, Lisa Ferraro Parmelee, and Anne Beaumont from the AEI Press for their editorial contributions. Special thanks to the National Research Initiative for supporting this project.

# Preface

In 1974, Robert Martinson, an adjunct assistant professor at the City College of New York, published an article entitled, "What Works: Questions and Answers about Prison Reform." In it, he summarized the results of a three-year project—Effectiveness of Correctional Treatment (ECT)—which reviewed the effectiveness of 231 offender rehabilitation programs that had been evaluated during the prior thirty years (see also Lipton, Martinson, and Wilks 1975). Based on his analysis of what was the most extensive offender treatment database that existed at that time, he concluded that, "with few and isolated exceptions, the rehabilitative efforts that have been reported so far have had no appreciable effect on recidivism" (Martinson 1974, 25).

This was a scandalous declaration at the time—partly because of the conclusion Martinson reached, but also because he had the temerity to leak it beyond a small academic audience. Had he reported his findings in an academic journal and left it at that, few people would have concerned themselves with it. But Martinson released his findings through *Time*, *Newsweek*, and *60 Minutes*.

In the wake of Martinson's revelation, others rushed in to control the damage. By challenging the effectiveness of these social programs for offenders, he had rattled the "progressive" zeitgeist of the 1960s and '70s. Those with a vested interest in maintaining the status quo felt they had to prove Martinson wrong. But his conclusion was difficult to refute. Even his own colleagues—anxious to distance themselves from his findings—had trouble doing so with the data before them. The following year, they released their own analysis of the ECT studies concluding that "the field of corrections has not as yet found satisfactory ways to reduce recidivism by significant amounts" (Lipton, Martinson, and Wilks 1975, 627).

The phrase "nothing works" was and is commonly attributed to Martinson, and to this day he is singularly blamed for quashing the rehabilitation movement of that era in favor of punishment and incapacitation. A follow-up review of the literature conducted by the National Academy of Sciences in 1976 also drew negative conclusions concerning the effectiveness of offender rehabilitation programs, but Martinson remained the pariah. He grew angrier and more alienated, and a few years after taking his unpopular stand—although he had begun to waver—he took his own life.

This account would be tragic enough if it ended with Martinson's death. But there is another tragedy, one in which ideology is allowed to trump empirical evidence in the field of offender rehabilitation. To this day, Martinson is still portrayed as the purveyor of the "nothing works" sentiment. In the early stages of my own career, I, too, attributed this phrase to him, until I actually read his work and could find no mention of it.

Martinson's assessment of the offender rehabilitation literature was indeed negative, but it was also justified. And the passionate reaction against his findings—and against him personally—revealed a powerful bias in academic circles that encourages those who "prove" that these programs work and dismisses those who suggest otherwise as being opposed to rehabilitation.

In the course of conducting my own evaluations of offender rehabilitation programs over the past decade, I have come to appreciate Martinson's predicament. Most who enter this field do so with high expectations. After all, on the face of it, most offenders have been dealt a bad hand due to crushing poverty or poor parenting. At worst, they have made poor choices, and surely would mend their ways if only they had access to enlightened forms of treatment, vocational training, or educational programs. Yet an objective assessment of the research literature reveals that the majority of rehabilitative programs have little or no lasting impact on recidivism. The slogan "Treatment Works!"—the adopted rallying cry of Martinson's detractors—has little empirical support among the more rigorously designed evaluations of these programs. And the expansion of social programs for offenders, based more on ideology than on science, fails to serve the offenders and taxpayers they are supposed to benefit. Moreover, the tendency to overstate their effectiveness dampens public interest in searching for correctional options that can produce measurable, long-term changes in crime.

As a small step toward reinvigorating this debate, this monograph critically reviews the most common forms of offender rehabilitation programs, outlines their underlying assumptions about the causes of crime, and provides a contrasting perspective that emphasizes closer monitoring of offenders, indefinite community supervision (the removal of which must be earned), and increased personal responsibility.

# 1

# From Punishment to Justice to Treatment: How Did We Get Here?

*If a man will begin with certainties, he shall end in doubts; but if he will be content to begin with doubts, he shall end in certainties.*

—Sir Francis Bacon, 1605

In colonial America, criminals were treated in much the same way as they were in England at that time, with punishments ranging from lashings, confinement in stocks, and public brandings for minor offenses to hanging for more serious crimes—including theft (Mitford 1973). Incarceration was primarily reserved for those who were awaiting trial.

Many people are surprised to learn that the use of prisons as a form of punishment and rehabilitation was an American innovation. Just as the electric chair was more recently conceived as a humane alternative to the guillotine or the gallows, the use of prisons as a legitimate criminal justice sanction arose in reaction to colonial America's nearly exclusive reliance on corporal punishment and execution.

The original American prisons appeared in the 1820s in New York and Pennsylvania. Though the two states' models were not identical, both stressed the importance of hard labor and silence— the latter so as to afford the offender the opportunity to do penance for committing the crime that led him there. Thus was born the *penitentiary*—a term that remains in use today, though it now refers to a far different institution than the one established by the Pennsylvania Quakers almost two hundred years ago.

Given the somewhat barbaric reputation prisons have now, it may be difficult to appreciate how revolutionary their conception was. Alexis de Tocqueville's visit to the United States was prompted by his desire to tour prisons and talk with wardens, staff, and even inmates to see whether such an approach might be applied in France. In fact, Gustave de Beaumont and Tocqueville's report, *On the Penitentiary System in the United States and Its Application in France* (1833), was published two years before Toqueville's *Democracy in America* (1835).

But a surge in population in the United States between 1820 and 1850 was accompanied by a surge in crime. Penitentiaries that once housed inmates in monastic seclusion had to make way for more inmates, bunking three or four in cells that had been designed for one. Requirements of silence had to be abandoned, and outbreaks of violence prompted a return to cruel and unusual punishment to maintain order. By 1867, a report by E. C. Wines and Theodore Dwight (commissioned by the New York legislature) concluded that there was no longer a prison in America that operated with inmate reformation as its primary goal (see Rothman 1998).

Population growth was not the only factor behind this temporary ebbing of the rehabilitative ideal. Reformers also held the naïve belief that confinement alone could produce positive inner change—even as the conditions of confinement grew more horrific. As prison historian David J. Rothman put it, "The Jacksonian reformers had presumed that inmates would not be hardened criminals, but 'good boys gone bad,' who after a period of corrective training would go on their way, not to return again" (1998, 113). This tendency to underestimate the appropriate magnitude of response to criminal behavior has been endemic to the field of offender rehabilitation ever since.

After World War II, renewed optimism and wealth (combined with low crime rates) led to new reforms and redoubled efforts to establish a rehabilitative ideal. The American Prison Association changed its name to the American Correctional Association, guards became correctional officers, and an array of activities such as education and vocational training became "treatment."

In spite of a few bumps along the way, most correctional systems continued through the 1970s to experiment with rehabilitation and treatment in lieu of (or in conjunction with) punishment and incapacitation.

However, this presumed renaissance began to wane after a number of studies revealed that these well-meaning efforts appeared to have had little or no lasting effect on crime (see preface). And so, beginning in the 1980s, public opinion shifted once again in favor of limiting the scope of the criminal justice system to punishment and incapacitation.

### Now That We're Here, Where Are We?

It is impossible to presage how present-day attitudes and events might be construed historically, but there is evidence that public perceptions are once again cycling back in favor of treatment as the primary goal of the criminal justice system. Psychologists Nathanial Pallone and James Hennessy (2003) point to a series of large treatment initiatives in the United States over the past few years as evidence of what they refer to as the "Rebellion of 2000." One is California's Proposition 36, in which adults convicted of nonviolent drug possession offenses are given the option of participating in drug treatment in the community in lieu of incarceration. Another is a plan by the governor of New York State to reduce the length of prison terms for nonviolent drug offenders, replace mandatory imprisonment with treatment, and grant judges greater discretion in handling drug-related charges. The burgeoning drug-court movement allows drug-abusing offenders who complete a prescribed period of community-based treatment (in addition to satisfying other conditions) to have their charges dismissed or conviction records expunged. Even the former drug czar, General Barry McCaffrey, underwent an apparent conversion in his final days in office, recommending that the emphasis of the war on drugs should shift in favor of prevention and treatment (Wren 2001).

In this monograph, I attempt to demonstrate why this seemingly noble shift in philosophies is a dangerous trend that is based largely on a misrepresentation of the problem itself, as well as of the touted effectiveness of the proposed solutions.

## The Problem

The news media's obsessive coverage of horrific crimes has fostered inaccurate perceptions of the crime problem in the United States. Polls conducted by the Gallup Organization reveal that the general public consistently assumes that crime has increased in the current year, relative to the year before. But what are the facts?

Although there is no definitive source, the U.S. Department of Justice administers two major sources of national crime data: the Uniform Crime Reporting Program (UCR), operated by the Federal Bureau of Investigation, and the National Crime Victimization Survey (NCVS), operated by the Bureau of Justice Statistics.

The UCR collects information from approximately 17,000 city, county, and state law enforcement agencies on the crimes reported to them. The primary types of offenses tracked are homicide, forcible rape, robbery, aggravated assault, burglary, larceny-theft, motor vehicle theft, and arson. These data are typically compiled on a monthly basis to monitor local, state, and national trends in crime.

Whereas the UCR data are based on reported crimes and arrests, the NCVS compiles information from the victims themselves—regardless of whether the crimes committed against them were reported to local authorities. Interviews are conducted at six-month intervals among a nationally representative sample of roughly 50,000 households comprising nearly 100,000 persons. The survey focuses on rape, sexual assault, robbery, assault, theft, household burglary, and motor vehicle theft.

Most criminologists agree that these two national monitoring systems serve important complementary functions. The UCR is designed primarily as a criminal justice resource to aid in law enforcement planning and administration. However, not all crimes are reported to the police—especially if they are committed by an acquaintance of the victim, or, as is often the case with rape, if the victim perceives that reporting the crime will result in being stigmatized. On the other hand, the NCVS does not include homicide, where the UCR does; and the UCR includes crimes committed against any person or entity, whereas the NCVS only measures crimes committed against persons at least twelve years of age.

The advantage of using both these databases to measure crime in the United States has to do with the reliability of the trends identified. Subtle—or even spurious—variations that appear in one database but not the other may be artifacts of the methodology of that tracking system. Trends that appear in both databases, however, are more likely to reflect actual changes in crime.

Figure 1 (see appendix, page 81) shows trends in crime rates per 100,000 people (UCR) or households (NCVS) in the United States over the past decade. The parallel downward changes in the two indexes suggest that crime—both violent and property—has actually *decreased* during this time, despite public perceptions to the contrary—perceptions probably driven by the excessive coverage of the least typical, and most salacious, criminal events. Clearly, anecdotal accounts and empirical data can tell very different stories, and the problem with basing criminal justice policies on the former is one of the central points of this monograph.

There is another crime statistic, however, that has received even less public exposure: recidivism. Recidivism can be broadly defined as an offender's return to crime after being released from jail or prison, and it is typically measured by re-arrests or returns to jail or prison within a specified period of time. Since it is estimated that offenders are only arrested for about 10 percent of the serious crimes—and less than 1 percent of all the crimes—they commit, we can be fairly certain that official estimates of crime committed by former inmates significantly understate recidivism.

The Bureau of Justice Statistics (BJS, part of the U.S. Department of Justice) has conducted two national studies of recidivism. The first, published in 1989, was based on a three-year follow-up of state and federal prison inmates released in 1983; the second came out in 2002 and was based on a three-year follow-up of inmates released in 1994. Both studies were ambitious attempts to merge and standardize disparate state and federal databases to provide a periodic snapshot of recidivism among U.S. prisoners. They showed that against an auspicious backdrop of steady decline in national crime rates, the percentage of those re-arrested within three years of their release from prison rose from 62.5 percent among 1983 releases to 67.5 percent among 1994 releases—an increase of 8 percent. The greatest increases occurred among those who had been initially sentenced for property, drug, and public-order offenses. Re-arrests rates among violent offenders showed the smallest increase among those released in 1983—59.6 percent, versus 61.7 percent for those released in 1994.

Overall, the BJS study found the highest rates of re-arrest for those originally incarcerated for motor vehicle theft (78.8 percent), buying and selling stolen property (77.4 percent), and burglary (74 percent). Ironically, and certainly counter to what one might glean from the evening news, those sent to prison for the most egregious crimes, such as homicide or rape, typically had the lowest recidivism rates (40.7 percent and 41.4 percent, respectively).[1]

How can we account for an 8 percent overall rise in the recidivism rate among released offenders while, at the same time, the crime rate in the general population is decreasing? Why is the specter of going to prison less of a deterrent to those who have been to prison before than for those in the general population? And, in light of the fact that most prisons in the 1990s tended to offer more rehabilitation programs than they did when the first cohort of prisoners was released in 1983, why do we not find lower recidivism rates among the 1994 releases?

Answering these questions requires that we look beyond the problem itself and take into account how we as a society have responded to it. Interestingly, the problem and the response are not opposing forces but, as I hope to demonstrate, have coalesced to justify the expansion of misguided solutions that come at significant financial and social costs.

## The Response

Public perceptions of what the priorities of the criminal justice system should be are notoriously cyclical. Moreover, these cycles seem to be anchored to high-profile events that (as shown above) often have little to do with actual trends. In any case, regardless of their empirical basis, public perceptions ultimately shape criminal justice policies.

In fairness, public opinion in this area is not always based on atypical events. More stringent drug laws passed in the 1990s resulted in dramatic increases in the proportion of state and federal prisoners who were committed for drug offenses. From 1980 to 1995, drug law violators accounted for 30 percent of the increase in the state prison population and 68 percent in the federal population (U.S. Department of Justice, Office of Justice Programs 1997). Partly as a result of these stricter laws, it is now estimated that approximately 80 percent of state and federal inmates either committed drug offenses, were under the influence of drugs or alcohol at the time of their crimes, committed their crimes in order to support their drug use, or had histories of substance abuse (Center on Addiction and Substance Abuse 1998). Heightened public awareness of this trend has spawned a growing number of state-based initiatives designed to divert first-time drug offenders from prison to community-based substance abuse treatment.

The effectiveness of these diversion programs has yet to be established, but the will to expand the use of these and other alternatives to punishment appears to be detached from their objective outcomes (Farabee 2002). What is even more disconcerting is that many of the experts charged with evaluating these programs are themselves emotionally and professionally tied to demonstrating their effectiveness (see chapter 2).

The alchemy between the perceived urgency of reversing existing crime trends and the promise of effective rehabilitation programs has fueled the public's desire for nonpunitive, rehabilitative responses to crime. Consider these highlights from recent state and national surveys:

- Two-thirds of Americans feel that education and vocational programs are the best way to reduce crime (Peter D. Hart Research Associates 2002).

- Most Americans (63 percent) view drug addiction as a medical problem that would be better addressed through counseling and treatment than incarceration (Peter D. Hart Research Associates 2002).

- More than half of Americans favor spending money on social and economic programs to reduce crime, whereas less than one-third are in favor of spending more money on the criminal justice system (Flanagan and Longmire 1996, 69).

- In a survey conducted in Oregon, nearly 90 percent of respondents approved of increased use of (and spending for) mandated treatment for drug-involved inmates (Doble Research Associates 1995).

- According to another national survey commissioned by the American Civil Liberties Union (ACLU) in 2001, 40 percent of Americans believe that the primary purpose of prison should be rehabilitation rather than punishment, deterrence, or maintaining public safety.

In response to these views, politicians have begun to champion the expansion of programs in prison and, in some cases, the diversion from prison altogether for certain types of offenders. National-level data on the actual number of programs now in place—and their costs—are scarce. However, a Bureau of Justice

Statistics analysis published in 1999 (based on 1996 figures) found that inmate programs in state prisons for that fiscal year cost $1.2 billion, exceeding the costs of food service ($1.1 billion), utilities ($682 million), and transportation ($197 million; U.S. Department of Justice, Bureau of Justice Statistics 1999b).

The BJS report did not specify what constituted "inmate programs," although it should be noted that this category did not include medical treatment (which was estimated at $2.5 billion). However, based on previous meta-analyses designed to reflect the current state of offender rehabilitation programs in the United States (Phipps et al. 1999), the majority of current prison-based programs tend to fall into five categories: substance abuse treatment, education, employment, cognitive-behavioral treatment, and life-skills training.[2]

Few would argue against the intuitive appeal of these programs. According to the Arrestee Drug Abuse Monitoring (ADAM) program, 51–79 percent of adult male arrestees and 39–85 percent of adult female arrestees tested positive for at least one illicit substance in 2000. Among state prison inmates, 37 percent reported using alcohol at the time of their offense (U.S. Department of Justice, Bureau of Justice Statistics 1999a). Approximately 40 percent of state prison inmates had less than a high school degree or its equivalent, and about one-third of state prisoners were unemployed prior to incarceration (U.S. Department of Justice, Bureau of Justice Statistics 1993; 2000). Cognitive therapy seems justified as a means of enhancing inmates' acceptance of personal responsibility and heightening awareness of the impact of their behaviors. Life-skills training also seems in order, given that many inmates may not have learned how to balance a checkbook, use public transportation, set goals, or manage their time effectively.

But are they effective in reducing recidivism?

The most common answers to this question are generally along the lines of, "Some programs appear to be effective for some types of offenders, under certain conditions." While this could be construed as an appropriately cautious statement for a researcher to make, it is instead a reflection of the inconsistent outcomes of these programs, and the poor quality of their evaluations. In fact, in a congressionally mandated report on the effectiveness of correctional programs, University of Maryland researchers reported that "[m]ost of the operational funding to prevent crime, both Federal and local, remains unevaluated by scientific methods" (U.S. Department of Justice, Office of Justice Programs 1997).

Chapter 3 presents the evaluation findings for the most common types of correctional treatment programs. But before we examine the research, we must first examine the context in which these studies commonly occur, as well as how the preexisting beliefs of researchers can lead to predetermined outcomes.

# 2

# Research Methods:
# We Can "Prove" Anything

The preface of this monograph related the story of Robert Martinson, the researcher who reached the unpopular conclusion in 1974 that most of the correctional treatment programs at that time had no appreciable effect on recidivism. But Martinson levied another important criticism against the field that received far less attention. Although his disapproval focused on two aspects of the studies he reviewed—weaknesses in program implementation and bias in how these programs were evaluated—he clearly found the latter more frustrating.

Many of the studies in Martinson's review that reported positive results—that is, reductions in recidivism—were based on subsets of the experimental group, such as those who successfully completed the program (versus untreated offenders and dropouts), or those rated as "amenable" to treatment (versus untreated offenders and those receiving treatment but deemed "unamenable"). In other words, the studies only evaluated outcomes for what could be called the "cream of the crop"—offenders who were motivated and persistent enough to complete treatment—while ignoring the offenders for whom the treatment had been ineffective. Moreover, in the majority of these cases, Martinson found that when these others were not removed from the experimental group, the putative effects of treatment disappeared. Martinson went so far as to say, "It is possible that some of our treatment programs are working to some extent, but that our research is so bad that it is incapable of telling" (Martinson 1974, 49).

Unfortunately, as the protreatment rhetoric has steadily regained its intensity over the thirty years since Martinson published his grim appraisal, the quality of the research on which it is based has not. A subsequent review of correctional treatment research examined studies conducted from 1968 through 1996. All were coded for research quality, ranging from one (poor) to four (excellent). Regarding the effectiveness of therapeutic communities, boot camps, and drug-focused group counseling in reducing recidivism, the authors reported a moderate effect for therapeutic communities and nonsignificant effects for the other two interventions (Pearson and Lipton 1999). However, the validity of these findings is challenged by the quality of the evaluations that produced them. None of the studies reviewed earned an "excellent" rating. All of the boot camp studies were rated "poor." Of the seven therapeutic community evaluations, one was rated "good," three "fair," and three "poor." Of the seven studies of drug-focused group counseling, five were rated "fair" and two "poor."

Not long afterward, a report issued by the National Research Council regarding the literature on correctional drug abuse treatment concluded,

> A number of studies of prison-based programs seem to demonstrate positive post-release outcomes, including reductions in drug use and crime along with improvements in employment, when inmates who have gone through prison treatment are compared with those who have not. . . . However, research conducted to date has not yet convincingly demonstrated the effectiveness of prison treatment programs. Even in studies that find a significant relationship between completion of a treatment program and post-release outcomes, the overall positive effect is attenuated by inconsistent findings. Moreover, positive treatment outcomes may be attributable to selection bias (e.g.,

the high level of commitment of offenders who completed the program rather than the capacity of the program to change their behavior). (Manski, Pepper, and Petrie 2001, 8.16)

## Methodological Shortcomings in Correctional Treatment Studies

One reason for the lack of rigor among correctional treatment studies is that they occur in the "real world." In the natural sciences—and even in the social sciences—studies can be designed that control for possible confounding influences so the researcher can state with relative certainty that differences between the experimental and control groups are indeed the result of the intervention. The sine qua non of these studies is the randomized design, in which subjects are randomly assigned to an experimental or control group. Given a sufficient sample size, it can be assumed that the two groups are identical. Thus, any differences in outcomes that occur can be confidently attributed to the effects of the treatment.

Unfortunately, field-based evaluations of actual treatment programs are rarely implemented with such controls. Evaluators in correctional settings typically have little say in how the inmates are selected to participate in a treatment program or how the program is actually carried out. Furthermore, it is commonly argued that randomly assigning one group of offenders to receive treatment while denying it to another is unethical. This, of course, assumes that the program is beneficial.

The reluctance to use random assignment in the evaluation of offender rehabilitation programs, though understandable, reflects the pervasive a priori belief in the field that these programs are inherently effective. By contrast, clinical trials to develop medications routinely employ random assignment on the basis that without conducting such a rigorous comparison the effectiveness of the medication cannot be established. As a result of the cultural bias against withholding the presumed benefits of social programs from offenders, correctional program evaluators are typically forced to rely on quasi-experimental research designs, such as comparing those who participated in a program with those who refused to participate. Many studies fail to include any comparison group and simply report the outcomes for those receiving treatment. In the end, it is the offenders—and taxpayers—who pay the price of ineffective programs being allowed to flourish in the absence of empirical scrutiny.

Let us consider some examples. After reviewing the methodologies of five prominent prison treatment evaluations, researchers from the Federal Bureau of Prisons (U.S. Department of Justice, Federal Bureau of Prisons, Office of Research and Evaluation 1998) observed the following six common sources of methodological bias:

- *Lack of random assignment.* For practical and ethical reasons, random assignment of subjects to either a treatment or control group is rare. In the absence of a true experimental design, it is difficult to disentangle the effects of treatment from the characteristics of the inmates who choose (or are chosen) to enter treatment.[3]

- *Incongruent follow-up periods.* The failure to control for time at risk after release can have a significant impact on outcomes.[4] For example, the program participants in one evaluation were at risk for an average of 34.7 months, whereas the nontreatment groups were at risk for 41 months. A six-month differential in time at risk could plausibly account for higher recidivism among the comparison subjects. Disparate risk periods are also a problem when researchers do not account for the time a parolee spends in a controlled residential aftercare program for the first six to twelve months following release.

- *Use of dropouts as comparison subjects.* Because of the difficulty in identifying appropriate nontreatment comparison groups, researchers sometimes compare treatment graduates with those who drop out of the program or are removed for custody reasons. While the rationale of this approach is to contrast subjects by level of treatment exposure, it is confounded by other (often unmeasured) variables that are associated with program termination or completion. One program, for example, had a graduation rate of only 20 percent. It is highly unlikely that this small percentage can represent all those initially referred to the program.

- *Failure to use appropriate statistical controls.* In spite of using nonequivalent treatment and comparison groups, few evaluators incorporate appropriate statistical controls to ensure the comparability of the study groups. For example, controlling for group differences in age, education, and number of prior arrests would allow for more direct comparisons of groups in a quasi-experimental design.

- *Failure to account for aftercare selection bias.* In most cases, participation in community-based treatment following release from prison is voluntary. As a result, not all offenders who receive prison-based treatment opt for aftercare; and of these, not all remain in treatment for the recommended period of time (typically three to six months). Thus, it is likely that those who choose to continue to participate in treatment after they are released from prison—and do so for an extended period of time—differ from other prison treatment graduates who do not. There are many reasons parolees may decide to participate in aftercare: a commitment to self-change, the need for housing (among residential treatment participants), pressure from their field parole agents, and so forth. Because the potential reasons for choosing aftercare are diverse, statistically controlling for these intrinsic differences is a complicated, sometimes impossible, undertaking. Nevertheless, the bias associated with self-selecting into aftercare must be taken into account—if not in the analysis, then in the interpretation.

- *Poor follow-up rates for interviews.* Evaluation studies that include data collected through follow-up interviews also are subject to selection bias. Follow-up rates lower than 80 percent have been shown to result in positively biased outcome estimates (Nemes et al. 2002). One study reviewed by Pelissier and colleagues had an overall follow-up rate of 60 percent (U.S. Department of Justice, Federal Bureau of Prisons, Office of Research and Evaluation 1998). In addition, subjects who had been recommitted to prison were not interviewed.

These methodological shortcomings make a difference. The authors of a large-scale meta-analysis of treatment programs for juvenile offenders found that the type and quality of research designs were *more* predictive of the outcomes than were the actual interventions being evaluated (Wilson and Lipsey 2001). And the weaker the design, the more likely a study is to produce favorable results. In fact, in an article entitled "Does Research Design Affect Study Outcomes in Criminal Justice?" Weisburd, Lum, and Petrosino (2001) categorized sixty-eight correctional program evaluations according to a one to five scale of methodological rigor and compared the effect sizes obtained for each of the five groups of studies. Whereas the lower-quality studies tended to show relatively strong effects on recidivism, the most rigorous evaluations—those employing true experimental designs—showed an average effect size of zero. In other words, the evaluations that provided the most valid test of the efficacy of the programs being evaluated revealed that these programs had no effect on recidivism whatsoever.

The biased findings that result from poor research quality have contributed to a gross misuse of criminal justice resources. But the impracticalities of conducting research in correctional settings represent only one of several sources of bias. The others are more difficult to quantify, but still deserve mention.

## Other Sources of Bias

Opportunities abound to impinge on what is assumed to be the scientific process of evaluating offender rehabilitation programs and accurately reporting their results. In some cases, the resulting bias is unintentional, but often it occurs because of pressures exerted upon researchers that predispose them to deliver findings in support of a particular position. Two sources of such bias relate to dominant fixtures in the lives of academic researchers: funding and publishing.

**Funding-Related Bias.** Conducting a large-scale outcome evaluation of a correctional rehabilitation program is an enormous—and costly—undertaking. For statistical reasons (based on sample-size calculations that help ensure the study will be sensitive enough to detect a moderate effect of treatment should there be one), such an evaluation requires there be several hundred subjects in the treatment group and several hundred more in the comparison group. Because official records cannot adequately capture certain behaviors such as pre- and post-prison employment, drug use, or criminal activity, the subjects must be interviewed by trained interviewers. These interviews typically take place prior to program participation, and again at discharge. Next, since the ultimate goal of these programs is to reduce subsequent criminality, these same subjects must be tracked for at least one year after release and reinterviewed. At this point, since self-reported accounts of sensitive (and often illegal) behaviors cannot be assumed to tell the whole story, objective measures must also be collected, such as urine specimens, hair samples, arrest records, returns to custody, and so on. Now, two or three years after the study began, the analysis of the outcome data can commence.

It is no surprise, then, that most of the prominent evaluations in this field rely on funding from state or federal agencies or, in some cases, large foundations. Often, the same agencies or organizations that fund the evaluation also funded the project being evaluated. The stakes are high and, for obvious reasons, they are also personal. Politicians have hazarded their careers on providing favorable results—and researchers are expected to deliver them. In one case, as my colleagues and I began an evaluation of a statewide treatment initiative for substance-abusing prisoners, the governor at the time told us, "I know treatment works; what I need you people to do is *prove* that it works!" For researchers whose sole support is derived from extramural grants and contracts, the subtle (or in some cases not-so-subtle) preferences of the funding source are difficult to ignore.

**Publication-Related Bias.** Most of us have heard the expression "Publish or perish!" with reference to the mandate of academics. It is an accurate description. Not only do universities use the number and quality of journal publications as a yardstick to determine academic salaries and promotions, but funding agencies also focus on publications as a means of quantifying the productivity of prospective grantees.

The emphasis on publications has its advantages. Many projects have been funded to researchers who collected the data and produced nothing. In the university setting, publications demonstrate that the researcher is making contributions to the field. And, because most journals are subject to a "blind" peer-review process, the number of articles that are actually published says something about the quality of the researcher's work as well.

But the publication process has one very important drawback— an obsession with significance. I am, of course, referring to statistical significance, which bears no relationship to "meaningfulness." Let us imagine that we are testing the effectiveness of a new

allergy medication. As one of the outcomes, subjects in the experimental and placebo groups are asked to rate their symptoms on
a seven-point scale, with one representing no allergy symptoms
and seven representing severe symptoms. With a large enough
sample size, a half-point difference on this scale could be statistically significant, but at the same time clinically irrelevant. The
converse could also occur, where seemingly large differences
between the experimental and placebo groups do not meet the
threshold for statistical significance. Nevertheless, studies demonstrating statistical significance are *significantly* more likely to be
published than those that do not. And so, in the field of offender
rehabilitation, the multitude of studies that show no significant
effect of these programs are never seen.

The preference given to studies with statistically significant
findings is in many ways defensible. Statistical significance can
serve as a filter for poorly designed studies, or erroneous hypotheses, that out of sheer luck appear to reveal a trend. But the published studies are those that form the research literature, and this
literature is what (ideally) informs policy. It is at this level that the
problem with significance becomes clear.

If researchers must publish in order not to perish, and it is far
easier to publish significant findings than nonsignificant ones, how
should they deal with the results of an ineffective program—one in
which there was no statistically significant difference between the
treatment and comparison groups?

One way to find significance is to go mining. Recall Martinson's
frustration with the state of the research he reviewed in the 1970s,
and how the same problems were identified in reviews conducted
a quarter of a century later. Researchers who did not find a significant difference after comparing the treatment group with the non-
treatment group simply went on to make further comparisons that
were unplanned and unjustified—they "drilled down" to smaller
and smaller subgroups until they could find a significant effect. If
the program participants did no better than the comparison group
of inmates who did not participate in the program, the researchers
might ask, how did they compare to those who were kicked out of

the program or to those who refused to enter the program in the first place? Or, how did the program participants who completed the program *and* volunteered to continue in an aftercare program while on parole compare to those who dropped out? Even if the program being evaluated were ineffective, we would expect these atypical subsets of prisoners to perform better after they left prison than those who had been "weeded out" along the way.

These data-mining techniques are common in the correctional treatment field, and they misrepresent how well (or poorly) a program has actually performed. It is an approach that capitalizes on self-selection, in which the treatment group is pared down to the most amenable 10–20 percent of the original group while the comparison group is left intact. But now the researchers have a publishable study—one that lends further support to the nebulous claim that "this program appears to be effective for some offenders some of the time, under certain conditions."

It is important to keep in mind that treatment dollars are still being spent on the remaining majority of ignored treatment participants who did *not* complete treatment *and* enter and complete voluntary aftercare. Thus, it appears that some of the studies in this field—whether by implication or inference—have inflated expectations for the majority by emphasizing the outcomes of a self-selected few.

### Politics, Religion, and Programs

Another source of bias in the field of offender rehabilitation research results from a different type of self-selection: that of the researchers. Most researchers in the social sciences tend to hold liberal attitudes regarding the causes of social problems and how to solve them (Tetlock and Mitchell 1993). Political leanings in either direction need not interfere with the scientific process of studying crime and offender rehabilitation, but few would argue that such separation exists. Psychologist Steven Pinker made this observation with regard to the unpopularity of legitimate but unpalatable scientific findings:

> Sophisticated people sneer at feel-good comedies and saccharine romances in which all the loose ends are tied and everyone lives happily ever after. Life is nothing like that, we note and we look to the arts for edification about the painful dilemmas of the human condition. . . . Yet when it comes to the *science* of human beings, the same audience says: Give us schmaltz! (Pinker 2002, 423)

Whether we like it or not, our general perspectives on life shape our initial assumptions, and these assumptions influence how research questions are generated and how findings are interpreted. Tetlock and Mitchell (1993) asserted that justice research is particularly vulnerable to these initial assumptions, first, because of a strong liberal bias in the field and, second, because of the nature of the research itself. Specifically, these researchers argued that, "given the lack of standardized, widely accepted research methods and given the difficulty of replication in soft psychology, there are plenty of opportunities for unintentional biasing of results at the level of the individual study" (236).

Our personal beliefs and biases emerge in research in many ways and are particularly important in how we interpret findings. Robert J. MacCoun (1998), a social psychologist at University of California–Berkeley, described five prototypes of evidence processing: fraud, advocacy, cold bias, hot bias, and skeptical. *Fraud* is an intentional effort to alter or conceal evidence for personal benefit. *Advocacy* is the selective use of information to support a hypothesis, albeit without actively distorting the findings or concealing other relevant information. *Cold bias* refers to inadvertent bias that occurs even when the processor is trying to maintain objectivity. *Hot bias* is also unintentional, but directionally motivated (i.e., the judge wants a certain outcome), and *skeptical* refers to unbiased processing of evidence that may differ from that of other judges because of individual differences in what constitutes proof. In other words, perceptions of a skeptic may be based on certain normative or probabilistic grounds, but even these decision rules can vary across individuals.

These prototypes are probably not exhaustive, but they do provide a taxonomy for discussing the considerable differences in how researchers, criminal justice administrators, and policymakers process the often vaguely stated evaluation findings for offender rehabilitation programs.

From what I have seen among other researchers and in the offender treatment research literature, fraud is extremely rare. Unfortunately, so is skepticism. Virtually all program providers with whom I have interacted tend to view evaluation results from an advocacy standpoint, that is, disseminating the positive findings while downplaying the negative. This is understandable; most businesses operate this way. It is also understandable that evaluators advocate expanding programs or interventions that, in their experience, have demonstrated value in reducing recidivism. (This assumes that these evaluations were in fact credible.) But the wholesale advocacy of rehabilitation—such as that expressed by slogans like "Treatment Works!"—is an inappropriate role for evaluators, and it weakens the credibility of social scientists. In the field of offender rehabilitation, skepticism is in short supply. Those few who do give voice to their skepticism tend to be dismissed, if not demonized, as being opposed to rehabilitation. Thus, we have established a subculture in which "proving" that programs work is viewed as caring and just, while demonstrating otherwise is not viewed at all.

During the time that I was writing this monograph, I attended a presentation by the director of a large toxicology lab that specialized in conducting drug tests for law enforcement agencies. After describing the myriad ways in which two identical laboratories could produce different test results for the same urine specimen, he revealed that, unless the amount of the tested substance clearly exceeds their levels, many laboratories will report that the specimen is drug-free. Why would it be preferable to report a "barely positive" test as negative? His answer was painfully familiar. If he were to report that the drug test was positive, nobody would be happy. The person who tested positive will contest the findings, as will his attorney. It also means more work for the parole agent. To defend the results means having to appear in court and may even require allowing inspectors to come into his laboratory and scrutinize his work, and so on. But if he says that the drug test was negative, everyone is happy. In short, if we can "prove" anything, and the data allow for multiple interpretations, why cause trouble?

## Are These Problems Unique to Criminal Justice Research?

Unfortunately, examples of poor-quality research can be found in all disciplines, even the natural sciences. But the prevalence (and tolerance) of nonexperimental research designs in the field of offender rehabilitation is rather unique.

According to British criminologist David P. Farrington (2003), the quality of research in criminal justice tends to move through periods of "feast and famine." Two of the most noteworthy feasts occurred under the aegis of the California Youth Authority (CYA) from 1960 to 1975 and the National Institute of Justice (NIJ) from 1981 to 1988. During these periods, both of these agencies fostered a wealth of rigorous research activity. Farrington attributes these "oases" of discovery to the influence of a small number of key personnel in these agencies who were knowledgeable about social science research and aware of the importance of basing policy decisions on experimental studies rather than descriptive or correlational ones. However, as staff turnover increased in the agencies and the top positions became more politicized, the emphasis on experimental research gave way to a demand for quick and dirty evaluations that supported the broader objectives of these agencies' administrations.

Another important reason for the lack of rigor in criminal justice treatment research relates to the relatively independent evolutions of *criminal justice* (the practice) and *criminology* (the science). Unlike medical interventions, which are almost always developed and tested through a close collaboration between hospitals or clinics and universities, criminologists are typically recruited to evaluate existing interventions that have been developed by practitioners with little knowledge of criminological theory or related clinical literature (Shepherd 2003).

To be sure, there are other factors at play here that we may never be able to overcome. Among them is the difficulty of measuring change. Whereas medical research readily lends itself to quantitative measurement, criminal justice treatment interventions must often rely on "soft" measures such as self-reports. Even the so-called objective outcome measures such as arrests have been shown to represent only a fraction of the true outcome of interest—in this case, criminal activity.

Thusly hobbled, we watch with envy the strides made in medical research over the past two hundred years and wonder why we are still debating the effectiveness of programs that have haunted our correctional institutions for generations.

# 3

# A Review of Programs
# and Their Effectiveness

Before we summarize the research literature concerning the effectiveness of offender rehabilitation programs, we must address a more fundamental question: What is a program? The *Merriam-Webster's Collegiate Dictionary* (2002) offers little clarification for the use of this word in a rehabilitation context. The most pertinent definition for our purposes is, "A plan or system under which action may be taken toward a goal." This seems reasonable enough; an offender program is a plan—that is, treatment—designed for the specific goal of reducing recidivism.

Most programs have plans. Unfortunately, many of these plans lack empirical foundations or specific procedures for implementation. In truth, the vagueness of the word "program" accurately conveys the vagueness of the programs themselves. Programs can refer to anything from a year or more of group and individual counseling to placing "Just Say No" leaflets in a prison's recreation room.

Not all offender programs are ineffective. As we shall see, some appear to show some positive results. The key point is that an intervention, albeit "a plan or system under which action may be taken toward a goal," need not be effective to be a program. And, unfortunately in the criminal justice system, once a program is established, it need not demonstrate effectiveness to continue.

So which programs seem to work?

## A Brief Review of Reviews

Over the past few years, several systematic reviews of the offender program literature have been conducted. This is a good sign, especially since (as mentioned earlier) a recent synthesis by Wilson and Lipsey (2001) of 319 meta-analyses of psychological, behavioral, and educational research found that type of research design accounted for more variance in outcomes than the actual interventions being evaluated. Based on this finding, the authors warned that policy decisions should never be based on a single study—or even a small group of studies—given the broad range of methodologies employed.

Meta-analyses and systematic reviews in the field of correctional treatment can be general, or they may have a particular theme or focus. Three prominent examples of general reviews or meta-analyses in the field of offender rehabilitation are studies conducted by MacKenzie and Hickman (1998) at the University of Maryland ("the Maryland study"), Phipps et al. (1999) at the Washington State Institute for Public Policy ("the Washington study"), and Pearson and Lipton (1999) from the National Development and Research Institutes ("the NDRI study").

The Maryland study was conducted on behalf of the Washington State Legislature Joint Audit and Review Committee to review the effectiveness of twelve types of correctional programs offered by the Washington Department of Corrections. The Washington study was released one year later and also was prompted by a request from the Washington State Legislature to examine the effectiveness of correctional programming offered by the Washington Department of Corrections at that time. Specifically, this report examined drug abuse treatment, sex offender treatment, cognitive skills and moral reconation therapy, anger management, victim awareness, life-skills training, adult basic education, correctional industries, vocational training, and other work programs.

The NDRI study was actually entitled "The Correctional Drug Abuse Treatment Effectiveness" (CDATE) project, and was an ambitious effort to create a comprehensive database of evaluation research on a variety of corrections treatment programs for offenders in both institutional and community settings. In spite of its name, however, this project was not limited to an examination of drug treatment. In all, NDRI's CDATE database included over 1,500 studies of all kinds in which an experimental treatment was compared with a comparison or control group.[5]

The conclusions regarding the effectiveness of the various types of offender rehabilitation programs below are based upon the reviews I have just described. For the sake of organization, I have tried to categorize all the programs into the domains established earlier: substance abuse treatment, education, employment, life skills, and cognitive-behavioral. But I will begin this review with an additional category that targets high-risk youths: prison visitation programs. This is arguably the most powerful example of the gap between science and practice in the offender rehabilitation field—a misguided approach made even worse because it is directed toward our youth.

**Prison Visitation.** In the late 1990s, during one of my visits to a state-operated correctional facility for youth, I noticed a dozen or so boys and girls getting off a bus to enter the same facility. The street clothes they were wearing indicated that they were not wards of the state. In fact, most of them seemed quite excited to be there.

The youths were quickly escorted through the reception area and to an outdoor visiting area. Sitting together in groups of two or three, these excited young visitors listened with rapt attention as the older and worldlier wards shared tales of their tumultuous youths and their own criminal exploits. I was unable to overhear much of these conversations, but was dismayed to see that no other adult could hear them, either. These impressionable young visitors were entrusted to the wards and left largely unsupervised!

As I signed out of the institution, I asked a correctional officer about the young visitors. "They bring these kids in to see what's in store for them if they don't straighten out. It's a good program." I asked him how he knew it was a good program, and he said it just made sense.

For this correctional officer, and presumably for the correctional system in which he worked, this gut-level appeal appeared to be sufficient. Shortly after this incident, an article appeared that presented the results of nine experimental comparisons of prison visitation programs (Petrosino, Turpin-Petrosino, and Finckenauer 2000). In short, the authors found that these programs (such as "Scared Straight") tended either to show no deterrent effects or, in most cases, actually had harmful effects. In the studies reviewed, youths who participated in a prison visitation program showed a 1–30 percent increase in risk of negative outcomes, such as subsequent arrest, self-reported delinquency, or average number of days in detention, relative to those who did not participate.

I mailed copies of this article to the top administrators of the youth correctional agency. Both thanked me. I naïvely assumed that sharing this information must have prompted change. But two years later, I learned that the prison visitation program was still operating. I decided to bypass administration and attempted to reach the officer in charge of the program to inform him of the risks associated with what he was doing, but he never returned my calls.

**Substance Abuse Treatment.** The Office of Justice Programs of the U.S. Department of Justice (1999) has estimated that approximately one-third of state prison inmates and one-quarter of federal inmates participated in some form of substance abuse programming during 1997. Interestingly, over the 1990s there appears to have been a trend to phase out some types of substance abuse treatment, such as residential treatment and professional counseling, in favor of programs such as peer counseling and drug education.

Among prison-based substance abuse treatment programs, the most commonly evaluated is the therapeutic community (TC). The TC philosophy holds that substance abuse is not the main cause of the offender's problems. Rather, it is a symptom of a larger problem: the disorder of the whole person. Thus, the goal of a TC is to "habilitate" clients in a holistic fashion, emphasizing personal responsibility. Rather than attempting to change offenders through counselor-led, didactic presentations, TCs rely primarily on the residents themselves to effect change on the individual. After reviewing eleven evaluations of prison-based TCs, Phipps et al. (1999) reported in the Washington study that two of the TC programs showed clear evidence of an effect, three showed some evidence of an effect, three showed no effect, and three were inconclusive. The reviewers further recommended caution in interpreting this literature because the individual studies varied considerably in terms of their quality and conclusions.

In their review of six other types of prison-based substance abuse treatment programs, the Washington study found that one showed some evidence of an effect, while the others either showed no effect or were inconclusive. In addition, the reviewers stressed, the study of the one program that did show some evidence of an effect had a number of methodological weaknesses, such as not including treatment dropouts in the outcome analysis.

The NDRI review showed more favorable results for TCs, but no support for other types of prison-based substance abuse programs. Again, however, the reviewers noted the generally poor quality of studies in this area. As mentioned earlier, of the seven therapeutic community evaluations in the CDATE meta-analysis, only one was rated "good," with the remainder rated "fair" or "poor." Of the seven studies of drug-focused group counseling, none was rated "good," five were rated "fair," and two were "poor" (Pearson and Lipton 1999). This is not exactly a bedrock of scientific support; but, as we shall see, the problems with the substance abuse treatment literature are common throughout the field of offender rehabilitation research.

**Education.** Since state prison inmates have an average of eleven years of education, it seems reasonable to assume that providing them with adult basic education will increase their chances of finding employment upon release and, in turn, reduce their likelihood of returning to crime. This assumption has been made with regard to prison inmates in the United States for over one hundred years.

The murkiness of this literature can best be described with a quote from the Maryland study, whose authors came to the following conclusion based on their review of twelve recent evaluations of correctional education:

> Many of the educational evaluations were rated low . . . because the studies compared only participants or completers with others. No attempt was made to identify a reasonable comparison group or to compare the characteristics (such as sex, race, age, prior criminal activity, etc.) of the participants to the comparisons. As a result, we do not know what types of individuals entered and/or completed the educational programs. There is a good chance that volunteers for program participation are already at a lower risk for recidivism than others who were not willing or interested in obtaining education. Thus, in these situations, we cannot conclude that the educational program changed the offenders. Of the 12 available evaluations, five . . . studies were reasonably well conducted. . . . However, many of these did not use statistical tests, and those that did failed to produce significant findings. Furthermore, generally speaking, the effect sizes were moderate or low. (MacKenzie and Hickman 1998, 13)

Despite this negative assessment, the authors concluded that adult basic education "appears to be a promising strategy for reducing recidivism."

The Washington study arrived at a similar conclusion regarding correctional education programs. After reporting mixed findings with reference to a small body of studies—most of which employed weak research designs—Phipps et al. deemed adult basic education to be a "promising, but still unproven, crime reduction strategy" (1999, 63).

The NDRI meta-analysis also examined the effects of college coursework on recidivism. The most rigorous study of the twelve reviewed showed no significant effect, and some of the studies rated as "poor" and "fair" showed a modest effect. Overall, the average effect size was negligible.

**Employment.** The argument for offering employment assistance to offenders seems reasonable: Most inmates enter prison with spotty job histories, and few have the requisite education or skills to compete in the workforce. While few of us would support a policy that *gives* offenders jobs, most would agree that providing inmates with the skills and experience they need to find a job upon release makes sense.

The Maryland and Washington reviews found some support for vocational education programs. Both cited a randomized study by Lattimore, Witte, and Baker (1990) in which inmates assigned to a vocational program were less likely (36 percent) than those in the control group (46 percent) to be re-arrested within two years of release. But by and large most of the more rigorous studies produced mixed results, showing either no significant difference between groups or, in at least two studies, slightly higher recidivism among those who received vocational education.

But most of the studies, regardless of the direction of their findings, relied on the common tricks of the trade—capitalizing on selection bias, excluding inmates from the experimental group if they dropped out or were kicked out of the program, and so on. In spite of the poor quality of the research, the Maryland researchers optimistically concluded that "the preponderance of the evidence suggests that vocational programs are effective" (MacKenzie and Hickman 1998, 21). The Washington report, on the other hand, more soberly concluded that not only were the evaluations of vocational programs scarce, but those that existed "reported mixed results and most of the evaluations used fairly weak research designs making it difficult to generalize the findings" (Phipps et al. 1999, 66).

**Life Skills.** Also referred to as "social-skills programs," life-skills programs seek to provide inmates with basic information to help them navigate the challenges of daily life. These challenges include balancing a checkbook, setting goals, communicating with others, and maintaining proper hygiene and appearance. Here again, an intuitively appealing rationale lies at the heart of the endeavor: By giving these inmates the skills they need to engage successfully in society, we reduce their need to support themselves through illicit means.

Despite this appeal, neither the Maryland nor Washington researchers were able to find any credible evidence suggesting that life-skills programs reduced recidivism. The two evaluations that used a true experimental design (reported in the Washington State report) found *identical* rates of recidivism between those assigned to a life-skills program and those who were not. Even the least rigorous study included in their review, comparing completers with dropouts (which virtually guaranteed the researchers would find an effect), found no significant effect of life-skills programming.

The NDRI review found that some social-skills programs were moderately effective. However, the review included a larger number of studies than the Maryland and Washington State reviews, and, as perhaps was suggested by the reference to "social-skills programs" rather than "life-skills programs," appeared to differ in how it defined this approach. It is worth noting that the only study rated as "excellent" methodologically showed a negligible effect on recidivism. Taking into account the quality of the studies in this domain, the NDRI researchers concluded that social-skills programs were not effective in reducing recidivism (Pearson et al. 2002).

**Cognitive-Behavioral.** The cognitive-behavioral category of programs refers to an array of approaches designed to change the way offenders process information and perceive their environment— and themselves. These approaches are based on the belief that criminals tend to think differently than the rest of us.

I have seen evidence of this in my own experiences with inmates. One of the clearest examples arose when I was conducting a focus group with eight inmates who were within a few months of being released from prison. We were discussing life on the outside when one of the inmates, a white male in his mid-forties, began shaking his head and admitted that he was terrified of what would happen when he got out. When I asked him to explain, he said he already had two strikes on his record and he knew that if he were to commit one more felony he would be returned to prison for at least twenty-five years, maybe for the rest of his life. But his choice of words gave me some insight into how he perceived his situation. "I'm afraid I'm going to get caught up in the stupid shit again and they'll put me back in for life."

For most of us, the specter of spending the rest of our lives in prison would be enough to ensure that we would never commit another crime. But this inmate seemed to see himself as a helpless victim of circumstances. Where was his sense of personal accountability?

The noted clinical psychologist Stanton Samenow, one of the early proponents of cognitive-behavioral treatment for offenders, wrote, "Criminals cause crime—not bad neighborhoods, inadequate parents, television, schools, drugs, or unemployment. Crime resides within the minds of human beings and is not caused by social conditions" (Samenow 1984, 6). Even so, confusion remains among experts as to who or what is responsible for the crimes an individual commits.

The NDRI, Maryland, and Washington reviews provide evidence that cognitive restructuring may be more than just another intuitively appealing strategy to reduce recidivism. NDRI researchers reported that the seven cognitive skills programs in their review were effective at reducing recidivism, on average, from a 57.4 percent success rate in the experimental groups compared to 42.7 percent success rate in the comparison groups (Pearson et al. 2002). However, they did not find the other types of cognitive-behavioral programs that emphasized behavioral therapy, such as providing tokens or vouchers, to reinforce desired behaviors.

Both the Maryland and Washington reviews reported similar conclusions regarding the effectiveness of cognitive-behavioral treatment, although both groups of reviewers noted that many of the studies of "moral reconation therapy" (a form of cognitive-behavioral treatment) were conducted by the same people who developed the program.

**Faith-Based Programs.** In recent years, many of the regulations that used to withhold federal funding from faith-based programs for prisoners have been relaxed or modified. Because the research base for faith-based prison programs is still developing, I have not included this category of interventions as part of the formal literature review. However, a large-scale evaluation of the InnerChange Freedom Initiative, operating in the Texas Department of Criminal Justice (TDCJ), was released in 2003 and deserves some mention here—especially in light of the growing interest in faith-based approaches at the state and federal levels.

In 1997, Prison Fellowship Ministries began a faith-based pre-release program in Texas where inmates participated in Bible study, life-skills education, and group meetings—all conducted with an evangelical Christian orientation. A study conducted by the University of Pennsylvania's Center for Research on Religion and Urban Civil Society (2003) found that inmates who graduated from this program were significantly less likely to be re-arrested (17.3 percent) than inmates who had been assigned to a control group (35 percent).

Unfortunately, these dramatic findings were more the result of the devil in the details than the program itself. In fact, the faith-based group was actually *more* likely to recidivate than the control group (24 percent versus 20 percent). In an editorial for the online magazine *Slate*, Mark A. R. Kleiman (2003) of the University of California–Los Angeles provided the following step-by-step accounting of how things got turned around:

> InnerChange started with 177 volunteer prisoners but only 75 of them "graduated." Graduation involved

sticking with the program, not only in prison but after release. No one counted as a graduate, for example, unless he got a job. Naturally, the graduates did better than the control group. Anything that selects out from a group of ex-inmates those who hold jobs is going to look like a miracle cure, because getting a job is among the very best predictors of staying out of trouble. And inmates who stick with a demanding program of self-improvement through 16 months probably have more inner resources, and a stronger determination to turn their lives around, than the average inmate.

The InnerChange cheerleaders simply ignored the other 102 participants who dropped out, were kicked out, or got early parole and didn't finish. Naturally, the non-graduates did worse than the control group. If you select out the winners, you leave mostly losers.

Sound familiar? Such practices form the basis for the majority of criminal justice treatment studies. In fairness to the authors of this study, all of the numbers above appeared in their report. But the public was never privy to these messy details. Much to the contrary, the results were summarized in a *Wall Street Journal* editorial (June 20, 2003) with the simple title "Jesus Saves."

As we have seen throughout this chapter, few of these evaluations are of sufficient rigor to allow us to draw firm conclusions about program effectiveness. Still, unlike the other program domains reviewed here, some of the cognitive-behavioral approaches appear to hold promise. At the very least, their relative effectiveness may tell us something about where we should go from here.

First, however, there is still much to learn about why most of the programs we have reviewed appear to be so ineffective. If we can identify faulty premises in the existing efforts to rehabilitate offenders, then we can propose more effective and focused alternatives.

# 4

# Why Don't These
# Programs Work Better?

The insistence among some policymakers and academics upon combating criminal behavior with "progressive" approaches such as
talk therapy, psychodrama, and life-skills training reveals an
inexplicable blindness to the wealth of evidence showing these
programs do not work—and the ability to continue insisting
upon them is a luxury not found in the private sector. Consider
the following example:

Back in the 1980s, after two decades of steadily declining
sales, Coca-Cola launched a secret project to develop a sweeter
drink that would reclaim its market share from increasingly popular Pepsi-Cola. The new formula was a consistent hit in focus
groups and outperformed Pepsi by a six-point margin in preliminary blind taste-tests. And so, in 1985, New Coke was released
as "the boldest single marketing move in the history of the pack-
aged consumer goods business" and, ominously, "the surest move
ever made" (Pendergrast 1993). The result has been described as
one of the greatest marketing blunders in the history of corporate
America.

But a closer examination of this "blunder" reveals an impres-
sive pursuit of truth—the sort of pursuit that is sadly lacking
in the applied social sciences. At first, the top executives at
Coca-Cola fiercely defended their decision to switch to the new
formula. They knew that New Coke was a superior product—
after all, they had invested $4 million to develop it. Egos and
careers were on the line. But their sales data told a different

story. Within months, Coca-Cola headquarters was receiving 8,000 calls a day from outraged consumers; more than 40,000 letters poured in to protest the new product. The decision was made to offer both New Coke and Classic Coke, but New Coke sales plummeted as the classic formula triumphantly regained and exceeded its original market share. Finally, despite the clear rationale for developing it and the promising preliminary results, New Coke was removed from the shelves (Pendergrast 1993).

The lesson to be learned from this example is simple but profound. When the data refuse to cooperate with our hypotheses, we must decide whether we will develop and test a new set of hypotheses or stubbornly persist with the old ones. The choice between persisting with a given ideology in spite of empirical evidence versus following the data seems to be a function of how precisely the outcomes can be measured and how directly the impact of these outcomes can be felt. In the case of Coca-Cola, objective market-share reports and accountability to stockholders ensured that the company's top brass would eventually capitulate to the facts. It is a sad truth that if offender programs were taken as seriously as soft drinks, the field of offender rehabilitation would be generations ahead of where it is now.

Confronted with the lackluster results of our current attempts to reduce criminality through social programming, the first question we must ask is, "What is going wrong?" Our approach appears logical: Since offenders tend to be more likely than nonoffenders to be undereducated and underemployed, to lack basic life skills, and to abuse drugs, addressing these problem areas should result in reduced crime. But, as we have seen, these approaches are not producing the intended effects. At best, their effects appear to be modest and short-lived. The many plausible reasons for these poor results can be reduced to two general categories: the quality of program implementation, and the assumptions upon which these programs are based. Let us briefly examine both categories.

## Quality

No matter how well a program is designed, its effectiveness ultimately depends on how well it is implemented. As obvious as this
axiom may seem, the actual operation of any given correctional
program is rarely subjected to outside evaluation. As a result,
administrators—not to mention the general public, which pays
for these programs—should not assume that our rehabilitation
programs are the same in practice as they are on paper. My own
awakening in this regard occurred when I began to make random, unannounced visits to prison programs. Unlike the occa-
sions of my previous site visits, when I would sit in on engaging
group therapy sessions, on nearly half of my unannounced visits
the scheduled groups were not taking place. In some cases,
groups were hastily convened for my benefit, and I would be subjected to an hour of watching an untrained counselor try to
engage apathetic inmates in a group or class that had no clear
purpose or curriculum. Appalling as this account is, it is admittedly subjective—not to mention limited to the programs I have
personally visited. Can we assume that this is the norm?

Yes. Over the past decade, hundreds of correctional programs
(adult and juvenile) in North America have been assessed using the
Correctional Program Assessment Inventory (CPAI). The CPAI is
designed to measure how closely a correctional rehabilitation program adheres to generally accepted principles of effective treatment
in terms of implementation, client screening and assessment, types
of treatment offered, staff training, quality assurances, and so forth.

Recently, Gendreau, Goggin, and Smith (2001) summarized the
overall findings of the three largest CPAI surveys. The researchers
found that "while some excellent individual programs were dis-
covered through these surveys, the blunt truth is that 70 percent
of all programs 'failed' according to the CPAI." Some particularly
telling examples of specific program deficits included low intensity (frequency) of treatment, with some programs only taking
place several hours per week; emphasis on factors that have not
been shown to predict or cause crime, such as self-esteem,

depression, or anxiety; and staff who were hired with no relevant experience or training, with most lacking a university degree.

Rehabilitation programs that target characteristics that do not cause crime and operate at low intensity with poorly trained staff cannot be expected to have a lasting, positive impact on the offenders who pass through them. And they don't. But somehow the expectations remain high.

Another factor to consider is that prisons are exceedingly difficult places in which to provide treatment. A decade ago, two researchers associated with the Federal Bureau of Prisons recognized this problem and tried to make the case for a "confinement model" of incarceration, suggesting that rehabilitation be dropped as the primary goal of imprisonment (Logan and Gaes 1993). Instead, the researchers argued, "the mission of a prison is to keep prisoners—to keep them in, keep them safe, keep them in line, keep them healthy, and keep them busy—and to do it with fairness, without undue suffering, and as efficiently as possible." Accordingly, programs should be allowed insofar as they do not interfere with this proposed mission of imprisonment, with the justification that they keep inmates engaged in constructive activities and, therefore, facilitate prison management. These researchers candidly stated,

> Prisons ought not to impose upon themselves . . . any responsibility for inmates' future conduct, welfare, or social adjustment. These are primarily the responsibility of the offenders themselves, and perhaps secondarily a concern of some others outside the criminal justice system. (Logan and Gaes 1993, 261)

Just as an overemphasis on rehabilitation distracts prisons from performing their role of protecting us from prisoners and the prisoners from each other, the circumstances of incarceration can also interfere with treatment. Based on a review of prison-based substance abuse programs in the United States, my colleagues and I (Farabee et al. 1999) identified several common implementation issues for developing programs in correctional settings:

- *Client identification and referral.* In most prison systems, determining who gets what kind of rehabilitative programming is not a scientific process. Some type of program participation is commonly mandated for all offenders or, in many cases, the need for treatment is determined by the absence of any other useful purpose the inmates might serve. In the latter case, many programs are only available to those whose custody levels preclude them from performing grounds maintenance, doing low-level desk jobs or janitorial tasks, or holding other jobs. Comprehensive screening and assessment to determine who actually needs what kind of treatment is rare.

- *Recruitment and training of treatment staff.* As pointed out by Gendreau, Goggin, and Smith (2001), hiring and retaining qualified treatment staff is a challenge for most prison-based programs. This is largely a function of low wages, but it also occurs because prisons tend to be established in remote, rural areas where land is cheap and community resistance is low. As a result, the viable labor pool is often limited.

- *Redeployment of correctional staff.* Evaluations of community-based offender treatment programs suggest that staff turnover undermines program stability and effectiveness and is especially destructive when it occurs among senior staff and in newer programs (Harland, Warren, and Brown 1979; Petersilia 1990). Although turnover among correctional staff is not unique to prison-based treatment programs, the fact that it occurs by design is. Professional advancement for correctional officers typically requires frequent transfers to different yards or institutions. This lack of continuity affects the stability of the treatment environment.

- *Coercion.* Although not all participation in corrections-based treatment is involuntary, coercion undoubtedly plays a role in most prison treatment admissions. Much of the growth in criminal justice treatment is based on the widely accepted dictum that involuntary clients tend to do as well as, or better than, voluntary clients (Leukefeld and Tims 1988; Simpson and Friend 1988). While it has been demonstrated that clients referred to community-based treatment through the criminal justice system remain in treatment longer than those not referred (Collins and Allison 1983; Leukefeld 1988), the long-term implications of external versus internal motivation as they relate to treatment outcomes are still unclear (Gerstein and Harwood 1990; Wild, Roberts, and Cooper 2002).

  Unfortunately, the research literature regarding the effectiveness of coerced treatment offers little guidance. A recent review revealed considerable variation in findings, most of which could be attributed to inconsistent methodologies, including different program types, outcome measures, and measures of legal involvement or coercion (Farabee, Prendergast, and Anglin 1998). Furthermore, none of these studies assessed the clients' perception of coerced or voluntary status. Rather, involuntary status was typically inferred from the client's criminal justice status at the time of treatment admission. The result is a lack of data comparing treatment effectiveness of involuntary and voluntary clients in the criminal justice system.

- *Aftercare.* Although few clinicians or researchers challenge the importance of providing aftercare services to parolees, several elements in the criminal justice system temper the effectiveness of these sessions. First, since many prison-based clients enter treatment involuntarily, only a minority volunteer to continue once they are no longer required to do so. Even those who do enter a program may leave early. Second, many community-based providers are reluctant to admit parolees—particularly those with violent or sex offender statuses. And third, there is limited control over the type and quality of treatment available in a parolee's county of residence, making it difficult to ensure a continuum of care consistent with his or her in-prison treatment model.

Perhaps for these reasons, prison programs tend to be of lower quality than similar programs in the community. Indeed, a recent comparison of community- and prison-based substance abuse programs found that prison-based programs were of lower overall quality than their community-based counterparts. Moreover, a follow-up comparison three years later revealed that while the community-based programs tended to improve over time, the prison-based programs actually *declined* in quality (Latessa and Pealer 2002).

The "drift" that seems to occur in prison rehabilitation programs is by no means unique to this field. Policy decisions regarding most types of interventions—even medical treatments—are based on small studies of these treatments under closely controlled conditions. But there is a difference between *efficacy*—how well a treatment works under ideal study conditions, and *effectiveness*—how well a treatment works as it occurs in the real world (Wells 1999). We have seen that most existing efforts to reform offenders through social programs are not effective. Unfortunately, given that most of the seminal studies upon which correctional treatment initiatives are based are themselves poorly controlled and biased in their conclusions, we cannot even be sure of their efficacy.

## Assumptions

One of the most pernicious assumptions about other people's criminal behavior is that somehow the rest of us are responsible. Recently, the *New York Times Magazine* published an article entitled, "Life With Parole?" in which the author attempted to expose the criminal justice system—namely parole supervision—as the true culprit behind our nation's high recidivism rates (Gonnerman 2002). The author recounted the experiences of a thirty-seven-year-old parolee, John Scott, as he attempted to reintegrate into society after being released from his second stint in a New York state prison. Mr. Scott quit his job as a dishwasher after two months, on the grounds that the pay was inadequate and because having to work on weekends interfered with his social life. Shortly thereafter, Mr. Scott's girlfriend reported to his parole agent that he had physically abused her. Over the next few months, Mr. Scott tested positive for cocaine three times, missed one of his scheduled appointments with his parole agent, exceeded his curfew, and was arrested for selling drugs. He was finally returned to prison.

Who was responsible for this unhappy ending? Apparently New York's predatory criminal justice system. The author lamented, "People are spending years, sometimes decades, cycling in and out of parole offices and prisons, seemingly *unable to escape the grip of the criminal justice system*" (emphasis added). She further commented that "there may be no better sign that our criminal justice system is broken than a parole office where the new parolees already know the officers by name."

Was Mr. Scott really a victim of an overly vigilant criminal justice system? Notwithstanding the conclusions drawn by the author of the *New York Times* article, most of us would probably argue that Mr. Scott got what he deserved. But what if we reframed the question and asked if he were a victim of other environmental or social circumstances? What if we learned that he came from a poor family or had a limited education? Should he be held to the same standards as the rest of us? If not, are we not obligated to provide to him the programs necessary to address these problems while he is in custody?

These are all reasonable questions. Unfortunately, the answers are more often the products of political or philosophical thinking than of science. As a result, our response to criminal offenders in this country has tended to be based more on what we assume than on what we know. The rest of this chapter is devoted to what I consider to be the four most misguided assumptions about the causes of crime and how to address them.

*Misguided assumption no. 1: The causes of crime can be traced to a single explanation.* The simplicity of this assumption is appealing, but unfortunately everyone has a different idea of what this single explanation should be. As a result, we have programs to enhance self-esteem (Davis, Ray, and Sayles 1995), stop or reduce drug use (Anglin 1988; Inciardi et al. 1997; U.S. Department of Justice, Federal Bureau of Prisons, Office of Research and Evaluation 1998), increase education (Brewster and Sharp 2000), enhance job skills (Bouffard, MacKenzie, and Hickman 2000), increase empathy (Hagan, King, and Patros 1994), address childhood trauma (Whaley and Koenen 2001), and so on.

The appeal of these single-item explanations is further diminished when we examine them under the harsh light of objectivity. There is no reliable evidence linking low self-esteem to criminality. In fact, some studies have demonstrated that offenders have higher self-esteem than nonoffenders (Calhoun et al. 2000). Nor has illicit drug use been shown to convert nonoffenders into offenders; rather, drug use serves to intensify criminal activity among those who are already offenders (Farabee, Joshi, and Anglin 2001).

Regarding education and employment, it is important to stay mindful of the denominator. Low education and unemployment are in fact correlated with the likelihood of committing criminal acts, but most people with less than a high school degree are not criminals, nor are most people who are unemployed. And, in fact, if low education and unemployment were causes of crime, we would see the highest crime rates in the poorest countries. Yet according to the 2000 International Crime Victims Survey (Van Kesteren, Mayhew, and Nieuwbeerta 2000), which provides an overall measure of victimization based on the percentage of people victimized at least once during the previous year (by any of the eleven crimes covered by the survey), there does not appear to be a clear association between each country's per-capita income ranking (shown in parentheses below) and crime level. The highest crime rates were found in Australia (27), England (12), the Netherlands (18), and Sweden (11). Canada (24), the United States (5), Scotland (not available), Denmark (8), Poland (71), Belgium (19), and France (23) fell in the middle, and Finland (13), Spain (35), Switzerland (4), Portugal (49), Japan (7), and Ireland (14) had the lowest rates.[6]

As for empathy, a landmark study conducted by Zamble and Quinsey (1997) sought, among other things, to determine why a group of offenders did not recidivate. When asked, the largest percentage of the ex-offenders (41 percent) indicated that they were afraid of being returned to prison; another 34 percent cited fear of other negative consequences for themselves or their families. Not one of the ex-offenders interviewed said that they refrained from committing a new crime out of concern for the would-be victim.

So if there is no single "cure-all" for reforming our criminals, why not prescribe them all? At least one review of the offender treatment literature has shown that multifaceted programs are more effective than those that rely on a single approach—of the successful programs identified, 70 percent were multifaceted, versus 38 percent of the unsuccessful programs (Antonowicz and Ross 1994).[7]

But here we encounter another problem: defining the universe of "all." It is much easier to target a single cause, such as drug use, than to attempt to change all the factors that have been shown to be associated with crime. More than a decade ago, Don Andrews listed the interventions that would be needed to target the crime-causing, or "criminogenic," factors known at that time.

> Changing antisocial attitudes, changing antisocial feel-
> ings, reducing antisocial peer associations, promoting
> familial affection/communication, promoting familial
> monitoring and supervision, promoting identification

and association with anticriminal role models, increasing self control, self-management and problem solving skills, replacing the skills of lying, stealing and aggression with more prosocial alternatives, reducing chemical dependencies, shifting the rewards and costs for criminal and noncriminal activities in familial, academic, vocational, recreational and other behavioural settings, so that noncriminal alternatives are favoured, providing the chronically psychiatrically troubled with low pressure, sheltered living arrangements, changing other attributes of clients and their circumstances that, through individualized assessments of risk and need, have been linked reasonably with criminal conduct, and insuring that the client is able to recognize risky situations, and has a concrete and well-rehearsed plan for dealing with those situations. (1989, 15)

This list has been getting longer. A more recent study of incarcerated female offenders found that drug-abusing women reported high levels of need for housing, psychological counseling, education, job training, family support, and parenting assistance upon release. The authors concluded that "the provision of drug abuse treatment referrals to women in jail may not break the continual cycle of drug use and incarceration if other needs cannot be addressed" (Alegmano 2001, 798).

Consequently, insofar as we are willing to continue combating crime with social programs, we must choose between focusing on a single behavior that is correlated with crime (and hope that the relationship is indeed causal) or, as described above, we must intervene in virtually every aspect of the offenders' lives.

*Misguided assumption no. 2: Co-occurring behaviors must be causal.*
If drug use occurs at a higher rate among offenders than among the general population, can we assume that drugs cause crime? If high-frequency offenders are overrepresented among lower

socioeconomic classes, does that mean poverty causes crime? If inmates tend to have less education than nonincarcerated adults, can we conclude that low education causes crime?

These questions are obviously simplistic, but they unfortunately represent common wisdom among many policymakers and academics when it comes to offender rehabilitation. If two factors such as poverty and crime are highly correlated, the reasoning goes, then all we need to do is reduce one and the other will follow. And so, as we have seen, prisoners participate in various programs such as drug treatment, vocational training, and education.

But most drug users are not criminals, nor (as mentioned earlier) are most people who are poor or have less than a high school education. This misinterpretation of co-occurring events is a ubiquitous problem that arises in observational research. As social scientists Crano and Brewer put it, "The main problem with the evaluation of freely-occurring variables is that they usually have natural covariates; that is, the occurrence of the variable of interest is confounded by the co-occurrence of other factors that accompany it in nature" (Crano and Brewer 1986, 140). In other words, the correlation between drug use, unemployment, and low educational attainment on the one hand and crime on the other may well be the result of one or more other factors common to all of these.

This is not to say that programs should not be offered in prison. There is some evidence that keeping inmates engaged in programs or recreational activities reduces the number of infractions that occur inside the prison walls, consequently improving prison management (Prendergast, Farabee, and Cartier 2001). But this is a separate issue. If offering programs facilitates prison management and reduces incarceration costs, then we should continue to offer them— but not under the guise of reducing recidivism. And, by extension, we should also fund the most cost-effective ways of keeping inmates occupied.

*Misguided assumption no. 3: Offenders have had blocked access to opportunities, so we should provide these opportunities in prison.* A popular theory concerning the cause of crime is that certain segments of our population have been blocked from pursuing valued goals via licit means. Drawing heavily from the work of Emile Durkheim (1951), many of today's criminologists have applied the term *anomie* to describe the social disorder that occurs when groups or individuals do not have access to legitimate means of achieving desired goals. As a result, members of lower socioeconomic classes resort to crime.

In fact, this may have been true at some points in our history. Few would dispute that racism—whether through formal or informal policies—placed African-Americans and other minority groups at a disadvantage. But it has proved difficult to make a case for the effect of poverty or discrimination on crime beyond a rhetorical level. Why was there no surge in crime among Japanese-Americans after they faced severe discrimination during World War II? And if women tend to be poorer than men, why are they less likely than men to steal (Pinker 2002)?

Regarding socioeconomic levels, there is scant empirical support for the assertion that poverty leads people to commit crimes (Akers 1994). In fact, although upward mobility across generations tends to be a slow process, a recent study found that the majority of children from U.S. households falling in the lowest quintile of wealth move up by at least one quintile when they are adults (Charles and Hurst 2002).

*Misguided assumption no. 4: A program can produce significant, long-term change in an offender's life.* At the center of our ongoing failure to reform offenders is a convenient but naïve perception that a brief, episodic intervention can effectively "fix" offenders whose lives have been marked by chaos, impulsivity, and entrenchment in a deviant subculture since childhood.

We have seen in chapter 3 that the vast majority of programs currently operating in our prison systems have never been subjected to rigorous evaluation. We have also seen that most programs that have been evaluated appear to have had little or no measurable effect, and, among those that did, the effects have tended to be modest and brief.

Up to this point, most of this monograph has been devoted to analyzing the elements of these programs and delineating a rationale for why they are not effective. But this final assumption calls into question the very notion of "programs." Putting aside questions concerning the underlying theories of these offender programs, the appropriateness of their curricula, and the quality of their implementation, we must first question whether we should be offering programs in the first place.

It is my contention that the very notion of a "program" as a means of addressing a problem as profound and complex as crime renders any effort—however well-meaning—impotent before it begins. This is not to say that offender rehabilitation cannot be achieved, only that doing so will require a paradigm shift from quick-fix *programs* based on single-item explanations of crime to long-term *practices* that include consistent standards for parolees and closer postrelease monitoring, while placing the responsibility of rehabilitation on the offenders themselves. This general distinction between programs and practices has been described by Sherman and colleagues (U.S. Department of Justice, Office of Justice Programs 1997), who defined a program as a focused intervention (typically established with external funding) intended to change behavior, and a practice as an ongoing, routine activity that is established in the community.

In chapter 6, I will elaborate on this alternative approach, but I must first lay the foundation for my case by reviewing several domains of the criminological and psychological research literature.

# 5

# Broken Windows, Deterrence, and Choices

In 1982, political scientist James Q. Wilson and criminologist George Kelling published an article in *The Atlantic Monthly* in which they described how the failure to detect and punish relatively minor acts of deviance in a community can lead to conditions that foster more serious crimes. To illustrate, the authors used an analogy of a broken window. If someone breaks a window in a building and nobody repairs it, others will infer that no one is taking care of the building. Over time, others will throw more rocks and break more windows. Once all the windows are broken, others will assume not only that no one is in charge of the building, but that the same applies to the street on which it faces, making the street fair game for further vandalism and disorder. Eventually, law-abiding people will avoid passing through this area, families will move, shops will close, and a downward spiral will ensue. Small acts of deviance beget more acts, and the eventual outcome is a crime-ridden community.

The "broken windows" analogy is a compelling one, but it was hardly a stretch from one of the incidents that inspired it. In 1969, Phillip Zimbardo, a Stanford University psychologist, placed a 1959 Oldsmobile in a ghetto area of the Bronx and another on an affluent street in Palo Alto, California. On both cars, the license plate was removed, the hood raised, and the hazard lights turned on. The car in the Bronx was stripped and vandalized within a few days, while the car in Palo Alto was untouched for more than a week—until Zimbardo began pounding it with a sledgehammer.

Within short order, others started cheering and eventually joined in until the car was completely destroyed (see Montgomery 1996).

The outcome of Zimbardo's experiment leads us to wonder what might have happened if the first person to lay a hand on either car had been confronted by a police officer—or even a concerned citizen. What if the standards that seemed generally to have existed in the Palo Alto community where the second car was located had been enforced when Zimbardo finally decided to test them?

Unfortunately, this question was not addressed in the study, but we can glean some answers from the crime patterns that followed a decision by New York City's former police commissioner William Bratton to focus police attention on the petty street crimes that had previously been ignored. In 1994, the NYPD adopted an approach known as "order-maintenance policing" (OMP), the core of which was to combat low-level crimes. Suspicious-looking individuals were stopped and frisked, and arrests were made for such acts as drinking in public, panhandling, and public urination. Over the following few years, New York City's crime rate plummeted (more so than that of other major U.S. cities during that time). And the decrease was not just for minor crimes and low-level disorder; serious crimes—including gun violence—showed significant declines as well.

Detractors commonly point to declines in crime rates nationally during the same period as evidence that the crime reductions seen in New York City were likely the result of other factors, most notably the economy. But as we will see in the following chapter, the increased enforcement that the NYPD began in the 1990s was associated with crime reductions even after controlling for economic factors (Corman and Mocan 2002).

A 1999 survey of New York City arrestees revealed that Bratton's adoption of the "broken windows" approach was more than just an abstract policy change. Almost all of those surveyed were aware that the police had stepped up enforcement for low-level crimes, about half reported that they had stopped engaging in these activities or at least cut back, and two-thirds of these cited increased police presence as their main reason for doing so (Golub et al. 2003).

The broken windows theory remains controversial, mainly because—like most criminological theories—it is difficult to rule out the influence of other factors (Miller 2001). Various forms of the broken windows approach have been tried in other cities, but with inferior results. One explanation for this is that these other programs tended to focus too literally on repairing physical damage in communities, whereas the NYPD approach emphasized aggressive law enforcement (Montgomery 1996).

The dramatic results seen in New York City suggest that serious crime prevention can be achieved by targeting low-level offenses—in essence, holding people to higher behavioral standards. It is an intervention of consequences and accountability rather than of social programs and therapy. And it may even be better suited as an approach to supervising known offenders—probationers and parolees—in the community than as a general crime-prevention strategy.

There are three weaknesses to the broken windows approach to preventing crime in the general population: costs, the potential for infringement on civil liberties, and the problem of perceived risk. The costs associated with expanding the purview of law enforcement from serious crimes to all crime can be substantial. Add to them the costs of prosecuting the throngs of low-level offenders whose crimes would previously have been ignored, and it is not hard to imagine how a writ-large version of the broken windows approach can become a prohibitively expensive undertaking.

The second issue, concerning the infringement upon civil liberties, is commonly raised by critics of both liberal and conservative viewpoints. Bratton's initial test of the broken windows approach took place in the subway system while he was chief of New York City's transit police. One of the immediate fringe benefits he found from catching "turnstile jumpers" was that many of them also turned out to be carrying weapons or drugs. But civil libertarians warn that these "fortuitous discoveries" can lead to lower thresholds for what merits disorderly conduct.

The third issue concerns the importance of offenders' perceived risk of being caught. In his analysis of a 1997 National

Youth Survey cohort (a sample of over 9,000), Lance Lochner (2003) found that community-level measures of arrests and disorder were not significantly correlated with youths' perceived risk of being arrested.[8] However, he also found that individuals did adjust their perceived arrest risk based upon their own personal experience or that of their siblings. It was this personal risk, not that of actual arrest rates for the crime committed, that was predictive of subsequent criminal behavior.

These controversial aspects of the broken windows theory are less of a concern when dealing with probationers and parolees. Focusing on these known offenders rather than on the community at large allows for a more efficient use of resources, which in turn reduces costs. Civil liberties—particularly for parolees—are already partially suspended. Home visits, random drug tests, and curfews are staples of virtually every parole system. Consequently, the legality of directing aggressive law enforcement toward known offenders under community supervision—even if presently underused in some jurisdictions—is already established. Lastly, the application of the broken windows theory to probationers and parolees takes direct aim at an offender's personal perceived risk of detection.

Wilson and Kelling contend that there are two sources of disorder: offenders and physical (broken windows, graffiti, litter) disorder. We have seen that one of the reasons given for New York City's success relative to that of other cities that have implemented their own versions of the broken windows theory is that the NYPD targeted offenders rather than physical disorder. The rationale behind this monograph is to continue in this direction, but with known offenders rather than the population at large. The following chapter proposes such a model, as well as a number of systems changes that must accompany it.

# 6

# A New Model—Sort Of

The literature presented in this monograph supports three principles that I contend are critical to enhancing the effectiveness of offender rehabilitation.

First, crime is a choice, not an unavoidable response to a hopeless environment. Most offenders could have completed school, but didn't; most had held jobs in the past, but chose easier, faster money over legal employment. Further, although many of these offenders committed crimes while under the influence of drugs or to get more money for drugs, drug use itself is a choice (Heyman 2001; Sommers and Satel 2005). Moreover, the pervasive belief that these criminals essentially had no choice but to resort to crime and drugs conveys a profoundly destructive expectation to them and to future criminals that undermines their perceived ability to control their own destinies.

Second, most offenders give little or no consideration to the risk of getting caught for crimes they are about to commit. This is not because they don't consider the imposition of a prison sentence to be a negative experience; rather, it is because they know that the risk of getting caught is extremely low. In fact, one study comparing actual offense rates against lifetime arrest data among criminally involved heroin addicts found that these offenders were only arrested for about one out of every thousand crimes they committed (Ball 1991). The popular notion that most prisoners don't mind going to prison is untrue. There is evidence that inmates perceive prison as being less punitive than does the general population (McClelland and Alpert 1985), but I have never met an inmate who would choose to stay in prison if granted the right to leave.

Third, social programs have not and never will produce long-term changes in the behavior of career criminals. The majority of us grew up perfectly well without various programs to teach us how to act. We completed school, became employed, avoided drugs (or limited their use), and never resorted to crime. We followed this path for the same fundamental reason: The rewards of doing so outweighed the rewards of not doing so.

Granted, the early life experiences of some offenders are disturbing and, in many cases, heartbreaking. But, like the rest of us, offenders will not change as a result of workbooks, videos, or talk therapy. They will change when the rewards of a licit lifestyle outweigh the rewards of a criminal lifestyle. Crime is not the result of a deficit in social services.

It is a little humbling for us humans to realize that the fundamental principles of behavior are quite consistent across species. Rats, pigeons, monkeys, and humans respond to rewards and punishments in very similar ways. Unfortunately (in the case of criminal behavior), among the most difficult behaviors to extinguish are those that were initially established under a random variable interval reinforcement schedule—that is, behaviors that were reinforced, but only episodically. Ironically, according to behavioral psychologist B. F. Skinner (1974), behaviors that have consistently been reinforced in the past will cease more rapidly once they are no longer reinforced, relative to behaviors that were only reinforced on a random basis—all other things being equal. Continuous reinforcement is superior for *initiating* a behavior, but variable reinforcement is superior for *maintaining* the behavior once it is established. Hence, because most offenders are only apprehended for a small fraction of the actual offenses they commit, they are unlikely to be deterred from committing crimes just because their behavior is unrewarded or even punished on an occasional basis. (For a more detailed review of the complex effects of sanctions and rewards on criminal behavior, see Marlowe and Kirby 1999.)

Before going any further, let us briefly turn to the psychological research literature to explore the role of two concepts to which I have alluded in this section: expectations and deterrence.

## Expectations

In a classic study conducted by Stone et al. (1999), the authors set out to test the hypothesis that invoking negative stereotypes impedes the subsequent performance of those who belong to the stigmatized group. Based on a 1996 college survey by Sailes and other studies that showed that white students perceived African-American athletes as being less intelligent, while African-American students rated white athletes as being less competitive and showing less "athletic style," the investigators reasoned that African-Americans would perform worse at a task if it were framed as a measure of intelligence rather than natural athletic ability, whereas white students would perform worse under the opposite conditions.

To test this, forty African-American students and forty white students at Princeton University (all of whom were novices at golf) were invited to participate individually in a ten-hole putting-course task. Participants were randomly assigned to either a "natural athletic" or "sports intelligence" condition. In the first condition, participants were told that this putting task had been shown to be a strong measure of natural athletic ability. In the second condition, participants were told that this task had been shown to correlate with the ability to think strategically during an athletic performance.

As predicted, African-American participants performed significantly worse if they had been assigned to the sports intelligence condition than the natural athletic condition. In contrast, white participants scored significantly worse in the natural athletic condition than the sports intelligence condition. It is important to remember that the task was identical for subjects in both conditions; the *only* difference was how the task had been framed.

In a similar study, Aronson et al. (1999) sought to examine whether it was necessary for subjects to belong to a traditionally stigmatized group for their behavior to be affected by expectations. Twenty-three white males at Stanford University who had high scores on the mathematics section of the Scholastic Aptitude Test were asked to take an eighteen-item advanced mathematics test consisting of questions from the Graduate Record Examination. The participants were randomly assigned to one of two study conditions: stereotype and control. In the stereotype condition, participants were given two minutes to review a packet of newspaper articles about the exceptional math achievement of Asians and were told that the purpose of this test was to gain a better understanding of why Asian students traditionally outperformed other students on tests of math ability. In the control condition, participants were told only that the test was a measure of their math ability.

As predicted, white students who had been primed with the expectation of inferior performance solved significantly fewer math problems than those who were in the control condition (the means of problems solved equaled 6.5 and 9.6, respectively). Again, as in the first study, the task was identical; only the expectations varied.

The effects of negative expectations and labeling are often invoked as justification for opposing incarceration. The argument is simple: once we designate an individual to be a "criminal," he will come to identify with that label and act accordingly. Making matters worse, society's negative expectations for this offender will further limit his options and deepen his involvement in the criminal lifestyle. But if expectations make a significant difference in our behavior, it is worth considering the kinds of expectations we are conveying to current and potential offenders. When we lament that offenders are "unable to escape the grip of the criminal justice system" (see chapter 4) or—another common mantra— that "addiction is a disease," what kinds of expectations are we creating? More pointedly, when we rush to provide social programs to those who have *chosen* to break the law, we undermine our own efforts by fostering the misperception that the responsibility for changing an offender's behavior lies outside the offender himself.[9]

## Deterrence

In the field of criminology, deterrence refers to the prevention of crime by creating an imbalance between the perceived gains of committing an offense relative to the perceived costs (Decker, Wright, and Logie 1993). If an offender perceives the potential costs to be higher than the potential gains, he will make a rational decision not to commit the contemplated offense. For obvious reasons, proponents of societal explanations of crime tend to view deterrence as a misguided or naïve goal of the criminal justice system. But given that this basic tenet of classical criminology has persisted since the eighteenth century (originally articulated by Cesare Beccaria in Italy and Jeremy Bentham in England), shrugging it off in favor of treatment may be a bit premature.

Classical criminologists contend that the effectiveness of deterrence is determined by three components: certainty, swiftness, and severity. The more certain, swift, and severe a punishment is perceived to be for a given criminal act, the less likely it is that act will occur. Moreover, there appears to be a dual benefit to providing certain, swift, and severe punishment. Offenders who are caught and swiftly punished for a crime will be less likely to commit further crimes (this is called specific deterrence). But successfully apprehending and punishing offenders also serves as an example to the general public that deters them from committing criminal acts as well (general deterrence).

The logic of deterrence seems impeccable, but how then does one account for the fact that 67.5 percent of those released from prison return within three years? By definition, these inmates should have become "successes" from the deterrence perspective, in that they had been apprehended for their crimes and punished.

Part of the problem appears to be that even among apprehended offenders, the likelihood of detection for any given crime remains extremely low. In fact, research has demonstrated that those with little or no prior experience committing crimes have much higher estimates of the certainty of punishment than do chronic offenders. This "experiential effect" means that the more times an offender perpetrates a crime, the *lower* his or her perceived risk will be when considering a subsequent criminal act (Paternoster et al. 1983).

In spite of the rich rhetoric and enlightened discussion of "progressive" treatment alternatives for offenders, is it possible that such a blunt instrument as police enforcement can produce significant changes in behavior? A recent study conducted by the National Bureau of Economic Research sought to assess the contributions of increased felony and misdemeanor arrests to the substantial drop in crime in New York City between 1990 and 1999 (Corman and Mocan 2002). The authors found that for every one-percentage-point increase in arrests for each of five major crimes, there were the following declines: murder—0.6 percent; assault—0.4 percent; burglary—3.1 percent; robbery—2.4 percent; and motor vehicle theft—5.9 percent. These findings held even after controlling for economic changes in New York City over this period. The authors concluded that, while both economic and deterrence variables were important in explaining the decline in crime in New York City during this period, the deterrence variables were more important.

This study indicates that there is a linear relationship between the vigilance of law enforcement and reductions in crime. But there also is evidence that substantial reductions in crime can be obtained if a certain "threshold" in detection rates can be achieved. Using official crime records from the state of Florida, Tittle and Rowe (1974) found that for a deterrence effect to manifest itself, arrests must first reach a "tipping-point" in which the probability of being arrested for a crime is at least .30. In other words, from a psychological standpoint, offenders appear to be unlikely to consider the legal consequences of their behavior until the chances of being arrested for any given crime meets or exceeds 30 percent.

But even among offenders who are under parole supervision, a 30 percent certainty of arrest is a far cry from what we find in current practices. Zamble and Quinsey's (1997) study of offenders released from prison found that only about one-third said parole supervision posed any serious difficulties. In fact, 55.6 percent reported that they had broken the terms of their parole within the first week of release. More than two-thirds of the offenders who had restrictions on drug and alcohol use reported using alcohol within the first week of release; 61.4 percent reported using at least one illicit drug.

The immediacy, or celerity, of a sanction is also vital for shaping behavior. As James Q. Wilson (1997) pointed out, when raising children, we do not say, "Because [you've misbehaved], you have a 50-50 chance nine months from now of being grounded." Unfortunately, the criminal justice system has yet to reach even this absurd standard.

But there is one more aspect of the deterrence literature that has been largely ignored by lawmakers: severity. Over the past twenty years, state and federal lawmakers have passed a wave of strict sentencing laws—particularly for drug-related convictions—designed to increase the severity of punishment for these offenses and, presumably, strengthen deterrence. (In Texas, for example, possession of four grams of cocaine carries a prison sentence of five years to life.) However, both the research literature and the burgeoning prison population suggest that increasing the severity of punishment is an ineffective strategy for deterring drug crimes.

Although the basic concepts of classical criminology have been around for centuries, empirical examination of these concepts did not occur until the 1960s (Akers 1994). As is often the case in the social sciences, the majority of these studies simply confirmed common sense: Swift and certain punishment deters crime. But these studies also revealed that the third critical feature of deterrence—severity—had by far the weakest impact on deterrence. One study of a sample of active residential burglars found that the decision to commit a hypothetical break-in was not directly associated with the severity of the threatened penalty alone. Rather, the severity of punishment only came into consideration in combination with the perceived gains and the perceived likelihood of being caught (Decker, Wright, and Logie 1993). This reliable finding in the research literature suggests that our society's emphasis on punishment severity rather than certainty may be a costly miscalculation.

## An Alternative Approach

Historically, "fine-tuning" our criminal justice system has not produced any measurable reductions in recidivism (Morris 1998). To have an impact on this longstanding problem requires a dramatic rethinking of what rehabilitation really means. Rather than continuing to operate under the assumption that correlates of crime, such as low socioeconomic status and drug use, are actually causes of crime that should be addressed through social programs, we must accept no excuses. Instead of relying on social programs we should enhance the level of supervision through smaller parole caseloads and new technology.

Increasing the certainty of arrest to the deterrence "tipping-point" of 30 percent or more among the general population is an unreasonable goal. Most Americans would understandably reject the virtual police state that this approach would require; the costs would be prohibitive; and by targeting the population as a whole, a large share of law enforcement resources would be wasted on individuals who were unlikely to commit a crime in the first place.

However, this lofty goal might actually be possible if we were to narrow our focus to known, high-risk offenders: parolees. These released offenders would need to be monitored so closely in the community that they would run a significant and perceptible risk of being caught for any crime (or violation of parole conditions) that they committed. In addition, the role of parole agents would be solely to enforce the law among their caseloads, not serve as social service coordinators. Depending on whether the offender committed a new offense or merely violated the conditions of parole, the parole agent would have the discretion to levy one of a host of graduated sanctions, ranging from small fines to community service to sending the parolee back to prison. And, lastly, parole sentences would be indeterminate. Specifically, a parolee would have to earn his way off parole by demonstrating for three consecutive years that supervision was no longer necessary.

This proposal is admittedly extreme, but by now the reader should have an appreciation of the complexity of this problem and the futility of our continuing attempts to address it with pro-grams. Bringing about significant reductions in crime requires that we abandon perfunctory programs in favor of more intensive and long-term practices.

Producing lasting change among chronic offenders will require a commensurate level of change among the criminal jus-tice systems that supervise them. To accomplish this, I offer the following recommendations:

*Recommendation 1: Deemphasize prison as a sanction for nonviolent reoffenses and increase the use of intermediate sanctions.* Overall, 2,166,260 persons were incarcerated in state and federal prisons in the United States at the end of 2002. To reach that total, the states during that year added 30,088 prisoners, and the federal prison sys-tem added 6,535 prisoners—a growth of 2.6 percent in the nation's prison population. This was its largest annual growth rate since 1999—and more than twice the percentage increase (1.1 percent) recorded during 2001. Put differently, about 1 in every 110 men and 1 in every 1,656 women were sentenced prisoners under the jurisdiction of state or federal authorities at the end of 2002 (U.S. Department of Justice, Bureau of Justice Statistics 2003b).

As alarming as these statistics are, there would probably be lit-tle objection to the current emphasis on incarceration if it appeared to serve as a deterrent. Unfortunately, as I have indicated earlier in the chapter, this has not proven to be the case. Not only does prison serve as an ineffective deterrent, it is also an expensive one. In 2000, prison expenditures in the state and federal systems exceeded $32 billion. The average cost per prison inmate per day was $61, versus $10 a day for parolees under intensive supervision (Camp and Camp 2001). Even if we were to double the resources allocated for postrelease supervision, the costs would still be less than one-third of the cost of incarceration.

But the goal of this monograph is not to recommend that offenders be diverted from prison to community supervision for committing a crime in the first place, but rather that they serve a larger percentage of their overall sentence on parole.

Unfortunately, the trend over the past decade has been to require an offender to serve his or her entire prison sentence, thereby eliminating the role of parole agents in supervising the offender in the community. Between 1990 and 2000, the number of prisoners who were released without any conditions of parole more than doubled (48,971 versus 98,000; U.S. Department of Justice, Bureau of Justice Statistics 2001).

Furthermore, minor parole violations such as positive drug tests, missed parole appointments, and failure to observe curfews should be punished by using a graduated set of intermediate sanctions, rather than by returning the offender to prison.

"Intermediate sanctions" refers to a group of punishments that fall between regular community supervision and prison, such as house arrest, electronic monitoring, community service, and fines. Many of these approaches have been more popular in Europe than in the United States, but there have been some recent attempts to apply them here. Thus far, there have been few methodologically sound evaluations of these efforts (Tonry 1998). The research to date supports only the modest claim that they cost less than prison and do not appear to *increase* recidivism (Morris 1998). But there appears to be a renewed interest among the public and researchers alike to advance our knowledge in this area and expand its application (Petersilia 2003).

Community-based sanctions should not be regarded as lax alternatives to incarceration. Studies have shown that most inmates perceive intensive community supervision to be highly punitive (Crouch 1993). In 1989, Oregon established an intensive supervision probation (ISP) program that included frequent home visits, random drug testing, and mandatory employment and gave convicted offenders the choice to participate in ISP or serve their time in prison. One-third chose prison (Petersilia 1990). In fact, there is evidence that the more criminal justice experience offenders have, the *less* punitive they perceive prison to be relative to intermediate sanctions (McClelland and Alpert 1985).

With the shift from incarceration to community supervision, will we not lose the undisputed advantage of prison—incapacitation? It is true that incarcerating offenders makes us all safer in the short run. And there are certain types of chronic high-risk offenders whose criminal histories merit long prison sentences. However, although in 2002 about half (49 percent) of state prison inmates were sentenced for violent crimes, about a fifth (19 percent) were sentenced for property crimes, and a fifth (20 percent) were sentenced for drug crimes. During that same year, over half (57 percent) of federal inmates were serving sentences for drug offenses, and only 10 percent were in prison for violent offenses. Taken together, we can see that the majority of incarcerated offenders in the United States are serving sentences for nonviolent offenses (U.S. Department of Justice, Bureau of Justice Statistics 2003b).

Technical violations and nonviolent new offenses committed on parole should rarely result in a return to prison. Replacing reincarceration as a first resort with a graduated schedule of intermediate sanctions can reduce correctional costs substantially without compromising deterrence.

*Recommendation 2: Use prison programs to serve as institutional management tools, not as instruments for rehabilitation.* As I demonstrated in chapter 3, the most sophisticated evaluations of prison-based treatment programs show that such efforts have no effect on recidivism. Even less rigorous studies (which tend to indicate an effect even when one is not present) reveal only modest program effects that typically dissipate within a year.

This is not to say that prison-based programs should be abandoned altogether. Researchers Charles Logan and Gerald Gaes, drawing from their experiences working in the Federal Bureau of Prisons, held that many programs currently offered in prison, such as vocational training, education, recreation, and so forth, should be justified solely on the basis of providing constructive activities for the inmates, not rehabilitation:

> It is the duty of prisons to govern fairly and well within their own walls. It is not their duty to reform, rehabilitate, or reintegrate offenders into society. . . . Prisons

ought not to impose upon themselves, by inclusion in a mission statement, any responsibility for inmates' future conduct, welfare, or social adjustment. These are primarily the responsibility of the offenders themselves, and perhaps secondarily a concern of some others outside the justice system. They should not be declared the official business of prisons. (1993, 262)

Indeed, most prison administrators who advocate prison programs do so from an institutional management perspective rather than a presumption that they will have an impact on recidivism (DiIulio 1991). And this management perspective may be more than wishful thinking. There is evidence that inmates in prison-based therapeutic community programs have lower rates of infractions, and that correctional staff assigned to these units have lower rates of absenteeism (Prendergast, Farabee, and Cartier 2001), though more rigorous research in this area is needed before rendering a final verdict.[10]

So if these programs can effectively counter the tedium of prison life and help wardens run their institutions more smoothly, what is the downside? Because most of them are designed to serve the grander purpose of changing the lives of those who participate, they cost much more than simpler organized activities that may well produce the same benefits (with regard to prison management). Structured recreation and job assignments can keep inmates busy as well—and at no additional cost. In contrast, institutions running more intensive treatment programs—such as therapeutic communities—can require up to twice the number of staff as non-treatment facilities.

A final reason to remove rehabilitation as a goal of incarceration is that prison life is unique and cannot be easily generalized to life beyond the prison walls. Learning to manage one's anger, abstain from drugs, or retain a job are critical skills for many inmates, but they are unlikely to be acquired in a setting where movements are regimented, drugs are unavailable (or prohibitively expensive), and job duties are assigned rather than earned.

In fact, one of the primary reasons that discretionary parole has fallen out of favor in recent years is the recognition that parole boards are unable to determine whether an inmate is reformed based solely on his or her behavior in prison (Morris 1998). Didactic presentations in prison regarding abstinence from drugs and crime may provide the inmate with useful information, but research on the prevention of drug use relapse has demonstrated the importance of practicing one's newly acquired non-drug-use behaviors in real-life situations where the most powerful cues to relapse can be found (Monti and Rohsenow 1999). Consequently, the more time an offender spends in the community—assuming he is under close supervision—the more likely he will be to adopt and practice behaviors associated with a lawful lifestyle.

*Recommendation 3: Mandate experimental designs for all program evaluations.* As I mentioned in chapter 2, the more rigorous a correctional treatment study is, the less likely it is to show an effect of a program on recidivism. The consequence of employing weak methodologies to evaluate correctional programs—or not evaluating them at all—is that we must continue to support them out of faith. If we instead required that any publicly funded offender program be evaluated using true experimental designs, we would likely narrow the field of "promising" programs by 95 percent. Not only would this relieve taxpayers of the burden of supporting ineffective programs, it would also help researchers identify directions for future intervention research. We could be standing on the shoulders of giants rather than nervously looking over our own.

Randomly assigning inmates to a treatment or control group, however, is often considered unethical because the control group is "deprived" of treatment. Those who raise such objections reveal their own bias that programs are effective because they are, well, programs. But this is a dangerous assumption, not only because most programs are ineffective, but also because some well-meaning efforts have actually been shown to *increase* criminal behavior (see McCord 2003). Without the use of rigorous experimental research designs, such adverse effects will go unde-tected. This has been a surprisingly difficult point to make with judges, correctional administrators, clinicians, and even university-based institutional review boards (IRBs), which are charged with protecting the safety of research subjects. Researchers in these contexts often find themselves defending the use of experimental designs, but they would be wise to take the offensive. As researcher David Weisburd pointed out, "The burden here is on the researcher to explain why a less valid method should be the basis for coming to conclusions about treatment or practice" (2003, 352).

*Recommendation 4: Establish evaluation contracts with independent agencies.* On the face of it, recommendation 4 appears to be little more than bureaucratic tinkering, but correctly implementing it would revolutionize the way all government programs operate and survive. Currently, agencies in most states are allowed—or required by legislation—to issue solicitations for independent research organizations to evaluate programs developed and imple-mented under agency sponsorship. Once contracted, the evalua-tors report directly to this agency. By this mechanism, not only is the agency directly involved in the design and implementation of the evaluation, it is also responsible for determining how (and if) these findings will be disseminated, despite the preferences of the independent evaluator. Should the results of the program evalua-tion demonstrate problems in its implementation or fail to show that the program is effective, the report may be delayed or sup-pressed, and the evaluator is unlikely to be awarded subsequent evaluation contracts.

This arrangement is the equivalent of asking an employee to evaluate his own boss. It creates a quiet complicity between the agency and the evaluator, in that both now share the same goal of keeping all participants comfortable, avoiding bad news, staying away from controversy, and, if need be, protecting the source agency from criticism. Under these conditions, it is no surprise that, nationwide, those program evaluations conducted under state agency contracts have significantly higher effect sizes than the more objective research studies funded by federal agencies like the National Institutes of Health. As a result, we have allowed an inestimable number of costly programs to lumber along unchecked, unimproved, and only seemingly accountable.

Whether liberal or conservative, no one condones wasteful spending. And this is precisely what the current system of "pseudo-accountability" engenders. This could be easily remedied by requiring all state agencies to submit their requests for evaluations to a truly neutral state agency such as (in California) the Bureau of State Audits (BSA), or another similar agency with the skill and expertise to work both with the evaluated agencies and with the eventually selected evaluator.[11] In turn, this coordinating agency would issue the requests for proposals, review the proposals, and select the contractor based on technical merit. The evaluator would report directly to this coordinating agency, which—upon approving the reports—would distribute the findings to a preestablished list of stakeholders, circulating negative as well as positive findings. This "arm's-length" relationship would moderate the effect of agency administrators whose egos are involved in demonstrating that whatever they are doing works, and neither they nor their subordinates would be able to exert pressure on the evaluators because they would not control the contract funds.

Admittedly, this change would require that the oversight agency be expanded to oversee all evaluations contracted by state agencies, but some of these costs could be recouped by downsizing the agency-level contract management divisions. More importantly, we could finally accomplish what many mistakenly believe already occurs when we evaluate how our tax dollars are spent: accountability.

*Recommendation 5: Increase the use of indeterminate community supervision, requiring three consecutive years without a new offense or violation.* The ability to levy indeterminate parole sentences is essential for facilitating long-term behavioral change. Understandably, it is also controversial. Discussions of sentencing policies typically center on the full sentencing period covering time served in prison and under community supervision, with the understanding that only part of that sentence will be spent in prison (ranging from one-third to two-thirds of the entire sentence). Indeterminate sentences establish maximum sentences for certain crimes and then allow judges and corrections officials to have discretion over the offenders' actual time served. In the 1960s, attempts to issue indeterminate sentences were based on the rehabilitative ideal that this legal flexibility could be applied to motivate offenders to behave themselves in prison and to participate in the programs necessary for their rehabilitation. But the resulting leniency and the observed ineffectiveness of these programs led to a backlash in sentencing policies that emphasized mandatory minimums. Also, as mentioned earlier, these problems were further exacerbated by the inability of parole boards to determine which prisoners had been "rehabilitated" based upon their behavior in prison (Morris 1998).

But an indeterminate parole period avoids these pitfalls. First, unlike most indeterminate sentencing practices, where maximums are set and the actual time served is a function of in-prison behavior and program participation, an indeterminate parole sentence would *literally* be indeterminate or, more accurately, the duration of community supervision would be determined by the parolee's behavior in real world settings.

Second, rather than attempting to ascertain whether a prisoner is rehabilitated based on his behaviors in a controlled environment, the criteria for success on parole would be based on the *actual* behaviors we are trying to promote: desistance in crime, abstinence from drugs, pursuit of employment, and so on. If an offender believes that receiving counseling for drug use, anger management, or life skills will help him to achieve these goals, he is welcome to do so. In fact, some have suggested offering vouchers to parolees to cover the expenses of certain kinds of community-based treatment for offenders who believe they are unable to change on their own. But the parole agent should be concerned with the outcomes—the results of random drug tests, the incidence of criminal involvement, the attainment or avoidance of employment—not the process by which each individual arrives at them. As I have attempted to demonstrate above, expectations are critical, and conveying to the offender the false notion that he cannot assume responsibility for his own life is an inappropriate role for parole agents and a damning affirmation for offenders.

Open-ended parole supervision is not the same as a lifetime sentence. The key difference is that the length of the period of supervision would be tied directly to the parolees' behavior. As it currently stands, a parolee who violates the conditions of his parole will be returned to prison for a period of time up to the remainder of his original sentence. After serving out the rest of his term, he is released without the constraints of further supervision.

As of 2001, parolees spent an average of twenty-two months on parole (Camp and Camp 2002). If the goal of parole is to hold offenders accountable for their behavior for a long enough period to make a transition into noncriminal lifestyles, the community phase of an offender's sentence should be extended to a minimum of thirty-six months. National studies of recidivism show that two-thirds of those who recidivate do so within the first six months of release. The risk of reoffending then tapers off somewhat during the second year and plateaus by the end of the third (U.S. Department of Justice, Bureau of Justice Statistics 1989; 2002). To the extent we can assume that official crime records reflect actual crime, it appears that parolees who successfully complete three years of community supervision pose a substantially reduced risk to society relative to those completing less than two years (the current standard).

Therefore, a reasonable place to begin would be to require that parolees complete three years on parole without violating a single condition. Obviously, if a parolee commits another felony, he should receive a new sentence and begin the entire process again. The indeterminate aspect of community supervision that I am recommending, however, refers specifically to misdemeanors and parole violations, such as missing parole appointments, staying out past curfew, or testing positive for drugs. These infractions, punished through intermediate sanctions, should result in a "resetting of the clock" in which the three-year community-supervision period is reimposed. Under this approach, a parolee would be able to complete his period of supervision in only three years—if he chose to do so. Otherwise, the clock would be reset with every new infraction, and the supervision could continue indefinitely. In short, released offenders would be closely monitored until they demonstrated that such supervision was no longer necessary.

Aside from enabling us to base a determination of whether an offender is "rehabilitated" on his behaviors in the real world rather than in the confines of an institution, another advantage to this approach has to do with what we know about the trajectories of criminal activity over the life course. When it comes to derailing criminal careers, it turns out that age may be our most powerful ally. After our teenage years, there is a slow but steady decline in crime participation rates, with relatively few offenders persisting into their thirties. Unfortunately, those who buck this trend tend to remain highly active in their thirties as well, but even this incorrigible sub-group tends to call it quits in their early forties (Blumstein and Cohen 1987). So our goal is not to shadow these offenders for the rest of their lives; rather, it is to deter them from committing further crimes when their criminal propensities are at their highest.

*Recommendation 6: Reduce parole caseloads to fifteen to one, and increase the use of new tracking technologies.* According to recent national surveys, the 85 percent of parolees who are assigned to regular supervision have an average of 1.7 face-to-face contacts with their parole agents each month. This is no surprise, given that the average agent's caseload for regular parole is seventy-three to one. The 14 percent of parolees assigned to intensive supervision have an average of 5.6 face-to-face contacts each month with their parole agents, whose caseloads average twenty-five to one (Camp and Camp 2001). Obviously, the term *intensive* is a relative one. In contrast, a college student taking a single course will see his professor eight to twelve times per month.

Petersilia and Turner (1993) have reported that even the relatively subtle difference between regular and intensive supervision (as currently practiced) can be associated with improvements in detection rates for crimes committed by offenders while on parole. Unfortunately, many observers have pointed to the increased arrest rates cited in this and other studies as a reflection of higher crime rates, and evidence that intensive supervision does not work. This argument is a specious one, as it is unlikely that those offenders who were assigned to intensive supervision committed more crimes in response to being more closely supervised; rather, those who chose to commit crimes while under more intensive supervision were more likely to be detected.

Reducing parole caseloads will allow parole agents to accomplish what many people believe parole already does—closely monitor the offenders' behavior. Notwithstanding the protests of those who are actually caught and held accountable for a crime or violation they committed while on parole, the truth is that most parolees tend to view parole agents as more of a vague nuisance than an active threat. In Zamble and Quinsey's 1997 study of parolees, only 18.9 percent said that their parole agent had hindered them on the outside, and 35.1 percent said their agent had been helpful. In other words, the majority of parolees reported that their parole agent had neither hindered nor helped them while on parole. As the authors concluded, the effect of parole agents was found to be "generally trivial" (43).

Most parole agents would bristle at the use of the word *trivial* to describe the influence they hold over their charges. In fact, parole agents wield considerable power over parolees once they have detected a crime or violation. But most parolees' crimes and violations go undetected; and, as we have seen, effectively interrupting a criminal lifestyle requires more than a .01 probability of being apprehended for any one criminal act. Therefore, unlike others who have called for a reinvention of parole by increasing the provision of social services (Petersilia 2003; U.S. Department of Justice, National Institute of Justice 2000a), I contend that the goals of justice and rehabilitation would be better served by enhancing parole agencies' ability to monitor their charges and deliver swift, intermediate sanctions.

Reducing caseloads is an important step toward this goal. Incorporating new advances in technology is another. While still too new to have been widely evaluated, global positioning systems (GPS) are now being used to assist in the tracking of parolees. Unlike electronic monitoring, which only indicates if the offender has left his home, GPS monitors provide detailed information on where the offender actually goes. The offender is fitted with a non-removable ankle cuff and personal tracking unit (PTU), which relays data on its wearer's location from the Department of Defense's GPS satellites to an Internet-based database system. Then, using a Web browser, authorities can access a detailed map to determine where the offender goes.

An advantage of GPS monitoring is that it allows parole agents to enforce "exclusion areas," such as schools or the home or workplace of the parolee's victim. If the offender enters one of these areas, the GPS tracking system will detect and record that information. The system also allows law enforcement authorities to determine if a GPS-tracked offender was in the area at the time that a crime was committed.

The promise of new technologies, however, is only as good as the people who use them. A recent exposé on ABC News provided a disturbing reminder of this fact. The report involved a convicted rapist, Lawrence Napper, who had recently been paroled in Texas. Napper was fitted with a GPS tracker and told he was only allowed to be at home, work, or the parole office. Nevertheless, while still on parole, Napper kidnapped and sexually assaulted a six-year-old boy. Why did Napper believe he could get away with his crime? Like most offenders, he had learned from experience. A subsequent review of his GPS tracking data showed that Napper had logged a total of 444 violations prior to his offense—including spending time at the school where he had committed the rape that led to his original conviction. All of the warrants that had been issued for these violations had been withdrawn. The employee responsible for monitoring the tracking data reported that her administrators were reluctant to act on his violations because doing so would have been counted as a *failure of the system*. She later resigned in protest (ABC News 2003).

To succeed in altering criminal lifestyles will require a lifetime approach. Refusing to punish an offender for minor violations to make the system appear to work in the short run guarantees that it will fail in the long run. We will never know what would have happened if Lawrence Napper had been slapped with a substantial fine or a short jail sentence the first time he took a detour home to test the GPS tracking system, but we know what happened when his actions had no consequences.

**Financial Considerations.** A true cost-analysis of the proposal presented in this monograph is beyond its scope—or at least the scope of its author—and it would require making some assumptions that are difficult at this point to make. For example, how long would it take for the average parolee to complete three consecutive years without committing a new offense or violating the conditions of parole? Knowing that 67.5 percent of those released from prison in 1994 were arrested again within three years of release (see figure 2 in the appendix, page 82) certainly tempers our optimism (U.S. Department of Justice, Bureau of Justice Statistics 2002), but it is important to keep in mind that by increasing the likelihood that we can detect a crime, we are also reducing the likelihood that that crime will occur. And, in the broader sense, if we can force offenders to be "square" for a sustained period of time (at least three years), we can be reasonably confident that they have themselves identified enduring alternatives to drug abuse and crime.

# 7

# Conclusions

There is a bias among many academics that criminal justice professionals who actually interact with offenders on a daily basis know less about them than those of us who watch them from afar. Countering that notion is not to deny the importance of systematic, independent research, but rather to point out that correctional officers and probation and parole agents possess a wealth of knowledge about why offenders change; and it would be a mistake to dismiss these observations simply because they are ideologically inconvenient. The notion among parole agents that most offenders choose to continue committing crimes and could quit on their own without the aid of social programs is clearly at odds with what we are hearing from ivory tower experts. Consider the following statement from an experienced parole agent in California:

> When you've been in this business so long, you tend to realize that you can't really change these guys. I've been 18 years in law enforcement. I think my goal, basically, is—of course keep the community safe—safety—I think my goal is mainly if any of them are doing anything, to find out what they're doing and stop them from doing that. Prevention. We could do prevention if we had the numbers. (Lynch 1998, 854–55)

We would be surprised to hear such a baldly pessimistic statement coming from the lips of an "expert." Yet to discount it would require that we wave off eighteen years of the speaker's direct, face-to-face experience with the specific population for whose behaviors we are trying to find solutions. How then do we account for this schism between academic and "frontline" perspectives?

This contrast in views probably has more to do with selective perception than real differences between experiential- and research-based findings. As I have attempted to demonstrate in this monograph, there is an extensive body of research literature that directly challenges the purported effectiveness of social programs on recidivism, and supports such common-sense approaches as increasing deterrence through closer monitoring. Those who are ideologically inclined to address the problem of crime through social programs will draw upon the "Treatment works!" literature to support their claims. Those of us who advocate returning responsibility to the offender draw upon the classical criminological literature that suggests offenders make rational decisions to commit crimes and can therefore make a rational decision to abstain. But the perception that being protreatment is the inevitable result of familiarizing oneself with the relevant criminological and psychological research is a myth.

In chapter 4, I attempted to distinguish correctional programs from correctional practices. Both seek to change behavior, but programs tend to be limited in time and scope, whereas practices are ongoing, routine activities. Given that crime itself is an ongoing, routine activity, the futility of relying on programs rather than practices to address the problem of crime should be clear. But it isn't.

News accounts suggesting that the criminal justice system is destabilizing communities by arresting the offenders who live there are as common as ever (Harris 2003). Advancing the notion that these offenders are destabilizing their own communities and that they do so by choice is decried as "unprogressive." But as I have demonstrated in this monograph, people do not turn to crime because they experienced a lack of social programs, nor will the provision of social programs make them stop. We also have seen that the most rigorous evaluations of correctional programs show that the social program response to crime does not reduce recidivism. The program approach to crime has been a worthwhile experiment—again. But there is no stronger evidence to support it this time than there was when it last cycled in—and out of—popularity in the 1960s and '70s. To reduce recidivism, we must return to basic principles of behavior and do a better job of detecting crimes and swiftly applying sanctions. Change is possible without workbooks, videos, and group meetings.

James Q. Wilson, one of the most influential thinkers concerning criminal justice in our time, has pointed out that there are only two restraints on behavior—morality and law. As the moral restraints associated with family and traditional values deteriorate, the need for more formal legal restraints increases (Wilson 1995). This is not an exhortation to create a police state, but rather to increase the use of legal restraints on the small subset of our population that has demonstrated that such supervision is necessary. Given that the average criminal career lasts about ten years and about half of all crime is committed by only 6 percent of offenders, the target population for increased scrutiny can be substantially narrowed actuarially. The parole population is a good place to start.

But we are not only trying to change offenders. Facilitating changes at the individual level will require substantial changes at the systems level as well. My reference to the "criminal justice system" throughout this monograph has been a convenient misnomer that implies a closely knit coalition of state and federal corrections agencies that share an administrative structure, exchange information, and hold similar priorities. No such coalition exists. Moreover, even within individual state departments of corrections, institutional and community supervision divisions tend to function more like fiefdoms than collaborators. Such large, loosely organized systems are notoriously resistant to change (Ruth and Reitz 2003). This is one of the reasons I have focused on parolees (who currently account for only about 20 percent of all community-supervised offenders; Camp and Camp 2002) rather than all offenders under community supervision.

The practices I have recommended in this monograph are no less vulnerable to faulty implementation than the programs I described earlier. Parole agents may succumb to pressure from their administrators to be more lenient, caseloads can swell to the point of being unmanageable, and evaluators may also be tempted to prove that these recommended practices work. This drift in implementation can devastate even the best-laid plans and is most likely to occur when such initiatives are inadequately funded and put in place too quickly. Because of this ongoing threat, it is critical to move in cautious, incremental steps. I have had great difficulty selling the mantra of "Think Small" to legislators and agency administrators who are anxious to roll out programs at the statewide level without first debugging them in single pilot programs, but the resulting infidelity in how such programs are typically implemented prevents us from knowing if their rationale might have had some merit.

For this reason, I have ordered the six recommendations of this monograph to ensure that each newly adopted action follows logically from the one before:

1. Deemphasize prison as a sanction for nonviolent reoffenses and increase the use of intermediate sanctions.

2. Use prison programs to serve as institutional management tools, not as instruments for rehabilitation.

3. Mandate experimental designs for all program evaluations.

4. Establish evaluation contracts with independent agencies.

5. Increase the use of indeterminate community supervision, requiring three consecutive years without a new offense or violation.

6. Reduce parole caseloads to fifteen to one, and increase the use of new tracking technologies.

Recommendations 1 and 2 begin the process by generating cost savings through reduced reliance on incarceration as a form of punishment for certain types of nonviolent offenders and replacing "therapeutic" programs with less costly activities that will serve the same prison-management function. Recommendations 3 and 4 are designed to establish and maintain rigorous standards to evaluate the effectiveness of the subsequent steps—recommendations 5 and 6— which are practices, not programs.

The actual effectiveness of what I have proposed has yet to be tested empirically, though there is a wealth of tangential evidence that suggests that these ideas are worth trying. Importantly, if the proposals offered here do not produce reductions in recidivism, I would be the first to advocate trying something else. Persisting with programs and policies that have no scientific merit simply because they are consistent with one's general life view helps no one, and the fecklessness of most offender rehabilitation programs serves a painful and costly reminder that it is time to move on.

# Appendix

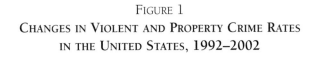

FIGURE 1

CHANGES IN VIOLENT AND PROPERTY CRIME RATES
IN THE UNITED STATES, 1992–2002

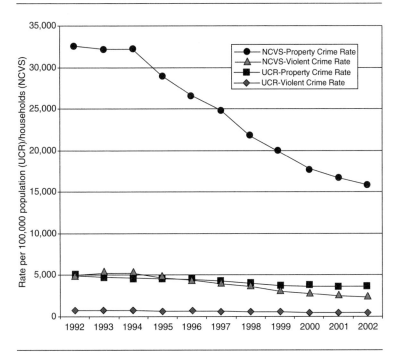

SOURCE: U.S. Department of Justice, Bureau of Justice Statistics 2003a; U.S. Department of Justice, Federal Bureau of Investigation 2003.

NOTE: UCR = Uniform Crime Reports; NCVS = National Crime Victimization Survey.

FIGURE 2

**PERCENT OF RELEASED PRISONERS RE-ARRESTED
WITHIN THREE YEARS, 1983 AND 1994**

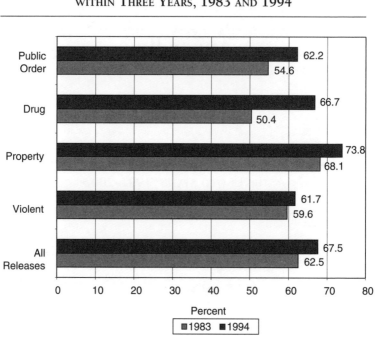

SOURCE: U.S. Department of Justice, Bureau of Justice Statistics 2002.

# Notes

1. It should be noted that these recidivism percentages apply to any crime committed by a previously incarcerated offender, not necessarily the same crime for which the offender had originally been sentenced.

2. The intent of this monograph is to examine programs targeting psychological and social problems. Psychiatric services for severely mentally ill offenders, as well as programs designed to treat sex offenders, are excluded from this overview.

3. Notable exceptions to this trend include Denise Gottfredson and Lyn Exum's 2002 evaluation of a drug court in Baltimore, and Harry Wexler et al.'s 1999 evaluation of a prison-based therapeutic community, both of which were based on experimental designs.

4. "At risk" refers to the time in which offenders are not incarcerated or otherwise confined so that they have opportunities to commit crimes if they choose to do so.

5. Another review conducted by Sherman and colleagues (U.S. Department of Justice, Office of Justice Programs 1997) included more than five hundred crime prevention program evaluations. This study was funded by the National Institute of Justice in response to a congressional mandate requiring the attorney general to provide a "comprehensive evaluation of effectiveness" of the more than $3 billion spent annually by the Department of Justice to support local crime prevention efforts. Although most of the report was devoted to nontreatment interventions, such as enforcement, incapacitation, and addressing general causes of crime, the authors did summarize the offender treatment literature, including preliminary findings from the NDRI study. They concluded that some rehabilitative programs can be effective in reducing recidivism, but doing so depends largely on the types of offenders, types of treatment, and how well the programs were actually implemented. The authors also pointed out the need for more information on measuring program quality, identifying specific criminogenic attitudes and characteristics, and

establishing minimum standards for delivering treatment pertaining to staff training, program size, program settings, and so forth.

6. Because the survey was limited to seventeen industrialized nations, the full spectrum of economic variability could not be captured. (GNI rankings taken from World Bank 2004.)

7. The authors also noted that they found only forty-four published studies in the period 1970–91 that were of sufficient rigor to be included in their review. Of these, fewer than half showed a statistically significant effect. As the authors reported, "Twenty effective programs in 21 years indicates that effective programs are truly exceptional" (98).

8. The broken windows theory would lead us to predict that those living in the most disordered communities would perceive themselves as being at the lowest risk of being arrested for any given crime.

9. Interestingly, although there are problems with many of the existing studies, the most effective class of interventions reviewed in chapter 3 involved cognitive restructuring. This approach emphasizes personal accountability and challenges illogical ("criminal") thinking rather than targeting co-occurring symptom behaviors associated with drug abuse, unemployment, lack of education, and so forth.

10. For example, current studies do not rule out the effects of selection bias in these programs. In some prison treatment programs, inmates with histories of violent behavior are ineligible to participate. In addition, inmates who fail to comply with program rules are often discharged from the program and sent to another unit, raising the possibility that lower levels of infractions among treatment participants are more aptly attributable to attrition than to the program itself.

11. Senate Bill 37 passed the California legislature with significant bipartisan support and was signed by the governor on May 7, 1993. As chapter 12, Statutes of 1993, it creates the Bureau of State Audits to replace the former auditor general's office, which closed due to budget reductions in December 1992. The bill transferred all of the auditor general's powers, duties, and responsibilities to the Bureau of State Audits. While the auditor general's office had been in the legislative branch of state government, the new Bureau of State Audits is in the executive branch. To ensure its independence, the law frees the bureau from the control of the executive and legislative branches. The state auditor is solely responsible for exercising the bureau's powers and duties, and its administrative operations are overseen by a state commission.

# References

ABC News. 2003. Eyes in the Sky, May 9.

Akers, R. L. 1994. *Criminological Theories*. Los Angeles, Calif.: Roxbury Publishing.

Alegmano, S. A. 2001. Women in Jail: Is Substance Abuse Treatment Enough? *American Journal of Public Health* 91 (5): 798–800.

American Civil Liberties Union. 2001. Most Americans Dissatisfied with Current Justice System. New York: ACLU, July 19.

Andrews, D. A. 1989. Recidivism Is Predictable and Can Be Influenced: Using Risk Assessments to Reduce Recidivism. *Forum on Corrections Research* 1 (2): 11–18.

Anglin, M. D. 1988. The Efficacy of Civil Commitment in Treating Narcotics Addiction. Special Issue: A Social Policy Analysis of Compulsory Treatment for Opiate Dependence. *Journal of Drug Issues* 18 (4): 527–45.

Antonowicz, D. H., and R. R. Ross. 1994. Essential Components of Successful Rehabilitation Programs for Offenders. *International Journal of Offender Therapy and Comparative Criminology* 38 (2): 97–104.

Aronson, J., M. J. Lustina, C. Good, and K. Keogh. 1999. When White Men Can't Do Math: Necessary and Sufficient Factors in Stereotype Threat. *Journal of Experimental Social Psychology* 35:29–46.

Ball, J. C. 1991. The Similarity of Crime Rates among Male Heroin Addicts in New York City, Philadelphia, and Baltimore. *Journal of Drug Issues* 21 (2): 413–27.

Beaumont, G. de, and A. de Tocqueville. 1833. *Du système pénitentiaire aux Etats-Unis et de son application en France*. Paris: H. Fournier Jeune.

Blumstein, A., and J. Cohen. 1987. Characterizing Criminal Careers. *Science* 237 (August): 985–91.

Bouffard, J. A., D. L. MacKenzie, and L. J. Hickman. 2000. Effectiveness of Vocational Education and Employment Programs for Adult

Offenders: A Methodology-Based Analysis of the Literature. *Journal of Offender Rehabilitation* 31 (1/2): 1–41.

Brewster, D. R., and S. F. Sharp. 2000. Educational Programs and Recidivism in Oklahoma: Another Look. *The Prison Journal* 82 (3): 314–34.

Calhoun, G. B., B. Glaser, T. Stefurak, and C. P. Bradshaw. 2000. Preliminary Validation of the Narcissistic Personality Inventory—Juvenile Offender. *International Journal of Offender Therapy and Comparative Criminology* 44 (5): 564–80.

Camp, C., and G. Camp. 2001. *The Corrections Yearbook 2000.* Middleton, Conn.: Criminal Justice Institute.

————. 2002. *The Corrections Yearbook 2001.* Middleton, Conn.: Criminal Justice Institute.

Center on Addiction and Substance Abuse. 1998. *Behind Bars: Substance Abuse and America's Prison Population.* New York: Columbia University.

Charles, K. K., and E. Hurst. 2002. *The Correlation of Wealth across Generations.* Cambridge, Mass.: National Bureau of Economic Research.

Collins, J. J., and M. Allison. 1983. Legal Coercion and Retention in Drug Abuse Treatment. *Hospital and Community Psychiatry* 34:1145–49.

Corman, H., and N. Mocan. 2002. *Carrots, Sticks and Broken Windows.* Cambridge, Mass.: National Bureau of Economic Research.

Crano, W. D., and M. B. Brewer. 1986. *Principles and Methods of Social Research.* Newton, Mass.: Allyn & Bacon Press.

Crouch, B. M. 1993. Is Incarceration Really Worse? Analysis of Offenders' Preferences of Prison over Probation. *Justice Quarterly* 10:67–88.

Davis, D., J. Ray, and C. Sayles. 1995. Ropes Course Training for Youth in a Rural Setting: "At First I Thought It Was Going to Be Boring." *Child and Adolescent Social Work Journal* 12 (6): 445–63.

Decker, S., R. Wright, and R. Logie. 1993. Perceptual Deterrence among Active Residential Burglars: A Research Note. *Criminology* 31 (1): 135–47.

Dilulio, J. 1991. *No Escape: The Future of American Corrections.* New York: Basic Books.

Doble Research Associates Inc. 1995. *Crime and Corrections: The Views of the People of Oregon.* Englewood Cliffs, N.J.: Doble Research Associates Inc.

Durkheim, E. 1951. *Suicide.* Trans. J. A. Spaulding and G. Simpson. New York: Free Press.

Farabee, D. 2002. Addicted to Treatment: Ideology Is Trumping Science in Our Quest to Rehabilitate Offenders. *Forbes*, December 23, 60.

Farabee, D., V. Joshi, and M. D. Anglin. 2001. Addiction Careers and Criminal Specialization. *Crime and Delinquency* 47 (2): 196–220.

Farabee, D., M. L. Prendergast, and M. D. Anglin. 1998. The Effectiveness of Coerced Treatment for Drug-Abusing Offenders. *Federal Probation* 62 (1): 3–10.

Farabee, D., M. L. Prendergast, J. Cartier, W. Wexler, K. Knight, and M. D. Anglin. 1999. Barriers to Implementing Effective Correctional Treatment Programs. *The Prison Journal* 79 (2): 150–62.

Farrington, D. P. 2003. A Short History of Randomized Experiments in Criminology. *Evaluation Review* 27 (3): 218–27.

Flanagan, T. J., and D. R. Longmire, eds. 1996. *Americans View Crime and Justice: A National Public Opinion Survey*. Thousand Oaks, Calif.: Sage.

Gendreau, P., C. Goggin, and P. Smith. 2001. Implementation Guidelines for Correctional Programs in the "Real World." In *Offender Rehabilitation in Practice*, ed. G. A. Bernfeld, D. P. Farrington, and A. W. Leschied. West Sussex, England: John Wiley & Sons, Ltd, 247–68.

Gerstein, D. R., and H. J. Harwood. 1990. *Treating Drug Problems. Vol. I (Summary): A Study of the Evolution and Financing of Public and Private Drug Treatment Systems*. Washington, D.C.: National Academy Press.

Golub, A., B. D. Johnson, A. Taylor, and J. Eterno. 2003. Quality-of-Life Policing: Do Offenders Get the Message? *Policing: International Journal of Police Strategies and Management* 26 (4):690–707.

Gonnerman, J. 2002. Life with Parole? *New York Times Magazine*, May 19.

Gottfredson, D. C., and M. L. Exum. 2002. The Baltimore City Drug Treatment Court: One-Year Results from a Randomized Study. *Journal of Research in Crime and Delinquency* 39 (3): 337–56.

Hagan, M. P., R. P. King, and R. L. Patros. 1994. Recidivism among Adolescent Perpetrators of Sexual Assault against Children. *Journal of Offender Rehabilitation* 21 (1/2): 127–37.

Harland, A., M. Warren, and E. Brown. 1979. *A Guide to Restitution Programming*. Working Paper 17. Albany, N.Y.: Criminal Justice Research Center.

Harris, S. D. 2003. Listening to Oakland: The City Is a Stark Example of How Tough Laws Are Putting More Seasoned Criminals on the Streets of California. *Los Angeles Times Magazine*, July 6, 12.

Heyman, G. M. 2001. Is Addiction a Chronic Relapsing Disease? In *Drug Addiction and Drug Policy*, ed. P. B. Heymann and W. N. Brownsberger. Cambridge, Mass.: Harvard University Press.

Inciardi, J. A., S. S. Martin, C. A. Butzin, R. M. Hooper, and L. D. Harrison. 1997. An Effective Model of Prison-Based Treatment for Drug-Involved Offenders. *Journal of Drug Issues* 27 (2): 261–78.

Kleiman, M. A. R. 2003. Faith-Based Fudging: How a Bush-Promoted Christian Prison Program Fakes Success by Massaging Data. *Slate*, August 5. http://slate.msn.com/id/2086617.

Latessa, E. J., and J. A. Pealer. 2002. Measuring Program Quality over Time—Examples from Three RSAT Programs. *Offender Substance Abuse Report* 2 (5): 65-66, 76-78.

Lattimore, P. K., A. D. Witte, and J. R. Baker. 1990. Experimental Assessment of the Effect of Vocational Training on Youthful Property Offenders. *Evaluation Review* 14 (2): 115–33.

Leukefeld, C. G. 1988. Opportunities for Enhancing Drug Abuse Treatment with Criminal Justice Authority. In C. G. Leukefeld and F. M. Tims, eds. *Compulsory Treatment of Drug Abuse: Research and Clinical Practice*. NIDA Research Monograph 86, DHHS Publication No. ADM 89-1578, pp. 328–37. Washington, D.C.: U.S. Government Printing Office.

Leukefeld, C. G., and F. M. Tims. 1988. Compulsory Treatment: A Review of Findings. In C. G. Leukefeld and F. M. Tims, eds. *Compulsory Treatment of Drug Abuse: Research and Clinical Practice*. NIDA Research Monograph 86, DHHS Publication No. ADM 89-1578, pp. 236–49. Washington, D.C.: U.S. Government Printing Office.

Lipton, D. S., R. Martinson, and J. Wilks. 1975. *The Effectiveness of Correctional Treatment: A Survey of Treatment Evaluation Studies*. New York: Praeger.

Lochner, L. 2003. *Individual Perceptions of the Criminal Justice System*. Working Paper 9474. Cambridge, Mass.: National Bureau of Economic Research.

Logan, C. H., and G. G. Gaes. 1993. Meta-Analysis and the Rehabilitation of Punishment. *Justice Quarterly* 10 (2): 245–63.

Lynch, M. 1998. Waste Managers? The New Penology, Crime Fighting, and Parole Agent Identity. *Law and Society Review* 32 (4): 839–69.

MacCoun, R. J. 1998. Biases in the Interpretation and Use of Research Results. *Annual Review of Psychology* 49:259–87.

MacKenzie, D. L., and L. J. Hickman. 1998. *What Works in Corrections? Report Submitted to the State of Washington Legislature Joint Audit and Review Committee*. College Park, Md.: University of Maryland.

Manski, C., J. S. Pepper, and C. V. Petrie, eds. 2001. *Informing America's Policy on Illegal Drugs: What We Don't Know Keeps Hurting Us*. Washington, D.C.: National Academy Press.

Marlowe, D. B., and K. C. Kirby. 1999. Effective Use of Sanctions in Drug Courts: Lessons from Behavioral Research. *National Drug Court Institute Review* 2 (1): 1–31.

Martinson, R. 1974. What Works? Questions and Answers about Prison Reform. *The Public Interest* 35:22–45.

McClelland, K. A., and G. P. Alpert. 1985. Factor Analysis Applied to Magnitude Estimates of Punishment Seriousness: Patterns of Individual Differences. *Journal of Quantitative Criminology* 1 (3): 307–18.

McCord, J. 2003. Cures that Harm: Unanticipated Outcomes of Crime Prevention Programs. *American Academy of Political and Social Science* 587 (May):16–30.

*Merriam-Webster's Collegiate Dictionary.* 2002. Springfield, Mass.: Merriam-Webster Inc.

Miller, D. W. 2001. Poking Holes in the Theory of "Broken Windows." *The Chronicle of Higher Education*, February 9, A14.

Mitford, J. 1973. *Kind and Usual Punishment.* New York: Knopf.

Montgomery, L. 1996. Broken Windows: How a Theory Shook the Foundations of Law Enforcement and Helped Heal a City. *On Patrol Magazine*, Fall.

Monti, P. M., and D. J. Rohsenow. 1999. Coping Skills Training and Cue-Exposure Therapy in the Treatment of Alcoholism. *Alcohol Research and Health* 23 (2): 107–15.

Morris, N. 1998. The Contemporary Prison—1965–Present. In *The Oxford History of the Prison,* ed. N. Morris and D. J. Rothman, 202–31. Oxford: Oxford University Press.

Nemes, S., E. Wish, B. Wraight, and N. Messina. 2002. Correlates of Treatment Follow-Up Difficulty. *Substance Use & Misuse* 37 (1): 19–45.

Nurco, D. N., J. C. Ball, J. W. Schaffer, and T. E. Hanlon. 1985. The Criminality of Narcotic Addicts. *Journal of Nervous Mental Disease* 173 (2): 94–102.

Pallone, N. J., and J. J. Hennessy. 2003. To Punish or to Treat: Substance Abuse within the Context of Oscillating Attitudes toward Correctional Rehabilitation. *Journal of Offender Rehabilitation* 37 (3/4): 1–25.

Paternoster, R., L. E. Saltzman, G. P. Waldo, and T. G. Chiricos. 1983. Perceived Risk and Social Control: Do Sanctions Really Deter? *Law and Society Review* 17:457–80.

Pearson, F. S., and D. S. Lipton. 1999. A Meta-Analytic Review of the Effectiveness of Corrections-Based Treatments for Drug Abuse. *The Prison Journal* 79 (4): 384–410.

Pearson, F. S., D. S. Lipton, C. M. Cleland, and D. S. Yee. 2002. The Effects of Behavioral/Cognitive-Behavioral Programs on Recidivism. *Crime and Delinquency* 48 (3): 476–96.

Pendergrast, M. 1993. *The Definitive History of the Great American Soft Drink and the Company That Makes It*. New York: Basic Books.

Peter D. Hart Research Associates. 2002. *Changing Public Attitudes toward the Criminal Justice System*. Washington, D.C.: Peter D. Hart Research Associates.

Petersilia, J. 1990. Conditions That Permit Intensive Supervision Programs to Survive. *Crime and Delinquency* 36 (1): 126–45.

———. 2003. *When Prisoners Come Home*. New York: Oxford.

Petersilia, J., and S. Turner. 1993. Intensive Probation and Parole. In *Crime and Justice: An Annual Review of Research*, ed. Michael Tonry, 281–335. Chicago: University of Chicago Press.

Petrosino, A., C. Turpin-Petrosino, and J. O. Finckenauer. 2000. Well-Meaning Programs Can Have Harmful Effects! Lessons from Experiments of Programs Such as Scared Straight. *Crime and Delinquency* 46 (3): 354–79.

Phipps, P., K. Korinek, S. Aos, and R. Lieb. 1999. *Research Findings on Adult Corrections Programs: A Review*. Olympia, Wash.: Washington State Institute for Public Policy.

Pinker, S. 2002. *The Blank Slate*. New York: Penguin Books.

Prendergast, M. L., D. Farabee, and J. Cartier. 2001. The Impact of In-Prison Therapeutic Community Programs on Prison Management. *Journal of Offender Rehabilitation* 32 (3): 63–78.

Rothman, D. J. 1998. Perfecting the Prison: United States, 1789–1865. In *The Oxford History of the Prison*, ed. N. Morris and D. J. Rothman, 100–116. New York: Oxford University Press.

Ruth, H., and K. R. Reitz. 2003. *The Challenge of Crime*. Cambridge, Mass.: Harvard University Press.

Sailes, G. A. 1996. An Investigation of Campus Stereotypes: The Myth of Black Athletic Superiority and the Dumb Jock Stereotype. In *Sport in Society: Equal Opportunity or Business As Usual?* ed. R. E. Lapchick, 193–202. Thousand Oaks, Calif.: Sage.

Samenow, S. E. 1984. *Inside the Criminal Mind*. New York: Times Books.

Shepherd, J. P. 2003. Explaining Feast or Famine in Randomized Field Trials. *Evaluation Review* 27 (3): 290–315.

Simpson, D. D., and H. J. Friend. 1988. Legal Status and Long-Term Outcomes for Addicts in the DARP Followup Project. In C. G. Leukefeld and F. M. Tims, eds. *Compulsory Treatment of Drug Abuse: Research and*

*Clinical Practice*. NIDA Research Monograph 86, DHHS No. ADM 89-1578, pp. 81–98. Washington, D.C.: U.S. Government Printing Office.

Skinner, B. F. 1974. *About Behaviorism*. New York: Vintage Books.

Sommers, C. H., and S. Satel. 2005. *One Nation under Therapy*. New York: St. Martin's Press.

Stone, J., C. I. Lynch, M. Sjomeling, and J. M. Darley. 1999. Stereotype Threat Effects on Black and White Athletic Performance. *Journal of Personality and Social Psychology* 77 (6): 1213–27.

Tetlock, P. E., and G. Mitchell. 1993. Liberal and Conservative Approaches to Justice: Conflicting Psychological Portraits. In *Psychological Perspectives on Justice*, ed. B. A. Mellers and J. Baron, 234–55. New York: Cambridge University Press.

Tittle, C. R., and A. R. Rowe. 1974. Certainty of Arrest and Crime Rates: A Further Test of the Deterrence Hypothesis. *Social Forces* 52 (June): 455–62.

Tocqueville, A. de. 1835. *Democracy in America*, ed. J. P. Mayer, trans. G. Lawrence. New York: Anchor, 1969.

Tonry, M. H. 1998. Intermediate Sanctions. *The Handbook of Crime and Punishment*, pp. 683–711. London: Oxford University.

University of Pennsylvania Center for Research on Religion and Urban Civil Society. 2003. *The InnerChange Freedom Initiative: A Preliminary Evaluation of a Faith-Based Prison Program*. Philadelphia: University of Pennsylvania.

U.S. Department of Justice. Bureau of Justice Statistics. 1989. *Recidivism of Prisoners Released in 1983*. Washington, D.C.: Government Printing Office.

———. 1993. *Survey of State Prison Inmates, 1991*. Washington, D.C.: Government Printing Office.

———. 1999a. *Prior Abuse Reported by Inmates and Probationers*. Washington, D.C.: Government Printing Office.

———. 1999b. *State Prison Expenditures, 1996*. Washington, D.C.: Government Printing Office.

———. 2000. *Correctional Populations in the United States, 1997*. Washington, D.C.: Government Printing Office.

———. 2001. *Prisoners in 2000*. Washington, D.C.: Government Printing Office.

———. 2002. *Recidivism of Prisoners Released in 1994*. Washington, D.C.: Government Printing Office.

———. 2003a. *National Crime Victimization Survey, 1973–2002*. Washington, D.C.: Government Printing Office.

————. 2003b. *Prisoners in 2002.* Washington, D.C.: Government Printing Office.

U.S. Department of Justice. Federal Bureau of Investigation. 2003. *Uniform Crime Reports.* Washington, D.C.: Government Printing Office.

U.S. Department of Justice. Federal Bureau of Prisons. 1997. *Key Indicators/Strategic Support System.* Washington, D.C.: Government Printing Office.

U.S. Department of Justice. Federal Bureau of Prisons. Office of Research and Evaluation. 1998. *TRIAD Drug Treatment Evaluation Project Six-Month Interim Report.* By B. M. Pelissier, G. Gaes, W. Rhodes, S. Camp, J. O'Neil, S. Wallace, and W. Saylor. Washington, D.C.: Government Printing Office.

U.S. Department of Justice. National Institute of Justice. 2000a. *But They All Come Back: Rethinking Prisoner Reentry.* By J. Travis. Washington, D.C.: Government Printing Office.

————. 2000b. 2000 Annualized Site Reports from ADAM. Washington, D.C.: Government Printing Office.

————. 2001. ADAM Preliminary 2000 Findings on Drug Use and Drug Markets. Washington, D.C.: Government Printing Office.

U.S. Department of Justice. Office of Justice Programs. 1997. *Preventing Crime: What Works, What Doesn't, What's Promising.* By L. W. Sherman, D. Gottfredson, D. L. MacKenzie, J. Eck, P. Reuter, and S. Bushway. Washington, D.C.: Government Printing Office.

————. 1999. *Substance Abuse and Treatment, State and Federal Prisoners, 1997.* Washington, D.C.: Government Printing Office.

Van Kesteren, J. N., P. Mayhew, and P. Nieuwbeerta. 2000. Criminal Victimisation in Seventeen Industrialised Countries: Key-findings from the 2000 International Crime Victims Survey. The Hague: Ministry of Justice, WODC.

*Wall Street Journal.* 2003. Jesus Saves: How President Bush Found Himself Hugging a Murderer in the White House. June 20.

Weisburd, D. 2003. Ethical Practice and Evaluations of Interventions in Crime and Justice. *Evaluation Review* 27 (3): 336–54.

Weisburd, D., C. M. Lum, and A. Petrosino. 2001. Does Research Design Affect Study Outcomes in Criminal Justice? *Annals of the American Association of Political and Social Science* 578 (November): 50–70.

Wells, K. B. 1999. Treatment Research at the Crossroads: The Scientific Interface of Clinical Trials and Effectiveness Research. *American Journal of Psychiatry* 156 (1): 5–10.

Wexler, H. K., G. De Leon, G. Thomas, D. Kressel, and J. Peters. 1999. The Amity Prison TC Evaluation: Reincarceration Outcomes. *Criminal Justice and Behavior* 26 (2): 147–67.

Whaley, A. L., and K. C. Koenen. 2001. The Juvenile-As-Adult-Criminal Debate. *Journal of the American Academy of Child and Adolescent Psychiatry* 40:619–20.

Wild, T. C., A. B. Roberts, and E. L. Cooper. 2002. Compulsory Substance Abuse Treatment: An Overview of Recent Findings and Issues. *European Addiction Research* 8:84–93.

Wilson, D. B., and M. W. Lipsey. 2001. The Role of Method in Treatment Effectiveness Research: Evidence from Meta-Analysis. *Psychological Methods* 6 (4): 413–29.

Wilson, J. Q. 1995. Crime and Public Policy. In *Crime*, ed. J. Q. Wilson and J. Petersilia, 489–510. San Francisco, Calif.: ICS Press.

———. 1997. Making Justice Swifter. *City Journal Autumn* 7 (4). http://www.city-journal.org/html/7_4_making_justice.html.

Wilson, J. Q., and G. Kelling. 1982. Broken Windows: The Police and Neighborhood Safety. *The Atlantic Monthly* (March): 29–38.

World Bank. 2004. World Development Indicators database. September. http://www.worldbank.org/data/databytopic/GNIPC.pdf.

Wren, Christopher S. 2001. A Drug Warrior Who Would Rather Treat than Fight. *New York Times*, January 8, B-9.

Zamble, E., and V. L. Quinsey. 1997. *The Criminal Recidivism Process.* Cambridge: Cambridge University Press.

# About the Author

**David Farabee**, PhD, is a research psychologist at the Neuro-psychiatric Institute's Integrated Substance Abuse Programs at the University of California–Los Angeles and a visiting professor at the Universidad Autónoma de Nuevo León in Monterrey, Mexico. He previously served as lead analyst for criminal justice research at the Texas Commission on Alcohol and Drug Abuse, and as assistant professor of psychiatry and research scientist at the University of Kentucky Center on Drug and Alcohol Research.